The Essence of Life's Invaluable Principles

Profound Answers to 60+ Questions

SIRSHREE

The Essence of Life's Invaluable Principles
Profound Answers to 60+ Questions
By **Sirshree** Tejparkhi

Copyright © Tejgyan Global Foundation
All Rights Reserved 2023

Tejgyan Global Foundation is a charitable organization
with its headquarters in Pune, India.

ISBN : 978-93-90607-90-7

Published by WOW Publishings Pvt. Ltd., India
First Edition published in December 2023

Printed and bound by Trinity Academy For Corporate Training Ltd, Pune

This book is the translation of the Hindi book titled,
"Jeevan ke Anmol Siddhaanton ka Saar" by Sirshree Tejparkhi

Copyright and publishing rights are vested exclusively with WOW Publishings Pvt. Ltd. This book is sold subject to the condition that it shall not by way of trade or otherwise, be lent, resold, hired out, or otherwise circulated without the publisher's prior written consent in any form of binding or cover other than that in which it is published and without a similar condition including this condition being imposed on the subsequent purchaser and without limiting the rights under copyright reserved above, no part of this publication may be reproduced, stored in or introduced into a retrieval system, or transmitted, in any form, or by any means, electronic, mechanical, photocopying, recording or otherwise, without the prior written permission of both the copyright owner and the above-mentioned publisher of this book. Any person who does any unauthorized act in relation to this publication may be liable to criminal prosecution and civil claims for damages.

Although the author and publisher have made every effort to ensure accuracy of content in this book, they hereby disclaim any liability to any party for any loss, damage, or disruption caused by errors or omissions, resulting from negligence, accident, or any other cause. Readers are advised to take full responsibility to exercise discretion in understanding and applying the content of this book.

To the true mentor,
who answers the questions that arise within,
and awakens the thirst for liberation!

Contents

Preface	9
Prelude	13
How to benefit from this book	17
PART I - Annihilation of the Mind While Dealing in the World	19
1. The Essence of Three Things	21
2. The Essence of the Utility of Things	23
3. The Essence of the Cause of Lies	26
4. The Essence of Preparing a Backup for Life	29
5. The Essence of Inner Beauty	33
6. The Essence of Undesirable Incidents	35
7. The Essence of Understanding Nature's Hints	38
8. The Essence of Being Aware Every Moment	40
9. The Essence of Solving Any Problem	42
10. The Essence of Watch, Wait with Wonder	45
11. The Essence of Happiness and Faith	48
12. The Essence of Need and Want	50
13. The Essence of Sad Incidents	52
14. The Essence of the Quality of Sleep	54
15. The Essence of Livelihood	58

16.	The Essence of Emotions	61
17.	The Essence of Freedom from Beliefs	64
18.	The Essence of Divine Occupation	67
19.	The Essence of the Highest Programming	69
20.	The Essence of the Final Tool	72
21.	The Essence of Challenges	75
22.	The Essence of Livelihood and Spirituality	77
23.	The Essence of Understanding Strict Laws	79
24.	The Essence of Creation Beyond Thoughts	81
25.	The Essence of Joy and Sorrow	84
26.	The Essence of Confusion and Clarity	86
27.	The Essence of Helplessness	89
28.	The Essence of Completeness in the Family	92
29.	The Essence of Information Received in Life	95
30.	The Essence of Parenting	98
31.	The Essence of Gain and Loss	100
32.	The Essence of Making the Right Decision	102
33.	The Essence of True Help	104
34.	The Essence of Discord in the Family	106
35.	The Essence of the Death of Loved Ones	108
36.	The Essence of the Impact of Words	110
37.	The Essence of Mental Stability	113
38.	The Essence of Freedom from Discord in Relationships	115

39. The Essence of Liberation from Sorrow	117
40. The Essence of Detachment	120
41. The Essence of Worldly Love	122
42. The Essence of Body Donation	124
PART II The Pure Essence Beyond The World	**127**
43. The Essence of the Eternal Experience	129
44. The Essence of an Egoist Mindset and a Wise Mindset	132
45. The Essence of Self-Experience Beyond the Ego	134
46. The Essence of Healing Injured Memories	137
47. The Essence of the Divine Form	139
48. The Essence of Divine Wisdom	141
49. The Essence of Polytheism	144
50. The Essence of Earthly Life	146
51. The Essence of Progress and Transcendence	148
52. The Essence of Sleep	151
53. The Essence of the Self	153
54. The Essence of Spiritual Knowledge	155
55. The Essence of Worthiness to Attain the Truth	158
56. The Essence of the Potential of the Human Body	160
57. The Essence of Breath as a Reminder	162
58. The Essence of Detached Action	165
59. The Essence of Spiritual Practice, Liberation, and Rebirth	168

60.	The Essence of Devotion, Quest, and Surrender	170
61.	The Essence of The Level of Spiritual Progress	172
62.	The Essence of the Guru	175
63.	The Essence of Practicing Knowledge	177
	Appendix	180-184

Preface

Ignite Your Quest to Find a Better You

"Why did the apple fall from the tree?" A student asked himself, and the answer that emerged within him led to the theory of gravity. He was none other than Sir Isaac Newton, the renowned physicist.

***

"How can I focus to see only the eye of the bird perching on the tree?" This simple yet potent question led Arjuna, the young Pandava prince from the Indian epic Mahabharata, to ascend the path to become the greatest archer of those times.

***

"Now death has come; what does it mean? What is it that is dying?" The teenager, Venkataraman, asked himself as he was overwhelmed with intense fear of death. His brave exploration of death revealed that he was not the body; he was the ever-present sense of being. He was transformed into the great spiritual master Ramana Maharishi.

***

When young Prince Siddhartha was deeply impacted by the sights of an old man, an ailing person, a dead body, and a radiant ascetic, he stumbled upon fundamental questions on the causes of suffering and the means to transcend them. He embarked on a quest to seek their answers and ultimately metamorphosed into Buddha – the Enlightened One.

***

"Was that true, or is this true? Was that a dream, or is this a dream?" asked King Janaka, the king of Mithila in the Indian epic Ramayana, when tormented by a vivid dream of destitution. This inquiry became the anchor for his journey of Self-discovery.

***

"Has anyone seen God?" Swami Vivekananda, the Indian monk and philosopher, would ask this question to all the saints or preachers he met. His quest finally guided him to his Guru, Saint Ramakrishna Paramhansa, the epitome of divine devotion.

***

Questions about the nature of true love, the essence of divine presence, and the purpose of existence led Persian poet and mystic Rumi to embark on his spiritual journey. His relentless questioning led him to a profound connection with the divine presence.

***

The above examples essentially show how curiosity and questioning have been instrumental in unraveling the profound mysteries of both material and spiritual realms since time immemorial. We must also become mindful of our questions and curiosities, lend them the right direction, reflect on them, and uncover the pearls hidden within them. This quest can begin with some simple, select questions.

These questions can shake one to their core and compel them to embark on a new journey. If you also have such questions, this book is the answer that will guide your curiosity and lead your quest to its culmination. By making the body instrumental, it will empower the quest to know, "Who am I?"

"Who am I?" is the most profound question in spirituality that has guided seekers of truth to their true nature to transcend the birth and death of their physical body. This question inspired the journey to Enlightenment for many Self-realized masters and their legends are a source of inspiration even today. This is the importance of asking the right questions, that draw the answers towards us. This is a sign of progress that keeps us steadfast on our chosen path in life.

Ponder for a moment: "How is my life today? Has it become valuable and important or is it in the process of becoming one, having attained the understanding of the Truth? What questions arise within me when I encounter day-to-day circumstances in my life?"

In our daily lives, when we face challenges, we often ask ourselves, "What should I do in this situation?" By doing so, the answers emerge from within. Such questions are important. When we question ourselves with the simple intention of finding their answers, we will be astonished to see how the answers reach us in unexpected ways - it could be through a person, a book, or an incident.

When we understand this, we will not feel distress in adverse situations, because we will be convinced, "I need to ask myself questions that awaken me and allow nature to play its part."

Just as a diamond shines after it goes through the process of chiseling and polishing, so too can we bring forth the best version of ourselves, our inherent nature, if we contemplate the right questions and embark on the path of progress.

This book covers the essence of more than 60 questions which hold the potential to enlighten our lives, provided we appropriately contemplate them.

This is the power of being aware of the right questions and the quest to find their answers!

Prelude

Demystifying the Two-Step Process of Human Evolution

Before diving into this book, let us grasp the value of questions and the importance of living by principles rooted in the essence of life.

Do the questions we ask ever cease?

It is important to know why you are asking a question. Questions aimed at solving a problem come to an end quickly. However, questions driven by a genuine quest for truth and the need for self-expression have fueled exploration across time. The insightful exchange between a Guru and a curious disciple has given rise to profound scriptures like the Upanishads. Thus, curiosity is the catalyst of progress.

Why do questions arise?

In the journey of life, breathing goes on, and so do hunger and thirst. Similarly, questions arise as a reflection of the human mind and its circumstances—a fundamental aspect of our nature. By being keenly aware of our curiosity and guiding it through contemplation, we can uncover hidden pearls of wisdom, enriching both ourselves and humanity.

Where do questions come from?

A child's curiosity about the whereabouts of his departed grandparents is natural. When he asks his father, "Where has grandpa gone?" his father gives him a make-believe answer, "Son, he has gone up in the sky; see that shining star!" The son innocently wonders, "Dad, when will you become a star?" His father playfully dismisses the question, knowing that time will unfold the answer as the child grows.

Likewise, when a disciple asks the Guru about his name and age, such inquiries prove fruitless; they cannot guide him further. Human progress lies in the cradle of simple yet profound questions that arise from the heart through a pure and unassuming mind.

The journey of questions and answers

Reflecting on our lives, we discover that time has unveiled answers to numerous questions, rendering many irrelevant. The queries we had as children, driven by fleeting curiosity, were eventually answered, revealing their relevance as we matured. As time progressed, the canvas of life expanded with education, work, marriage, children, relationships, health, and financial well-being, each contributing to the intricate tapestry of our existence.

Questions suggest that answers are within reach. When nature intends to communicate or bestow a gift upon us, it does so through the emergence of questions within us—through the spark of curiosity. The latter section of this book unfolds profound answers to life's questions born from such curiosity. It is not a chicken-and-egg scenario; it is evident that questions must come first, acting as curious hooks to draw out the answers concealed within them. This ongoing dialogue of questions and answers becomes the driving force behind human advancement.

Now, let us delve into the primary question that explains the title of this book.

What is the essence of life's invaluable principles?

Imagine someone asking you how life ought to be lived—amidst sorrow or joy, guided by hatred or love, in stress or relaxation, with a scarcity mindset or contentment. What would your response be? Of course, we know everyone's answer. This answer encapsulates the essence of life.

What kind of life do people lead today? A life filled with distress, trouble, stress, and a pervasive sense of scarcity. Every facet of life seems marked by a feeling of incompleteness and inadequacy because the focus has been on the tangible external world, rather than the hidden essence within. Prioritizing wealth, comforts, ego, and superficial appearances has led to these consequences. So, if you notice any shortcomings in your life, ask yourself, "What is the essence of this aspect of life, and what have I given undue importance to?" This question will guide you to the essence of your life.

Once you have understood the essence of every facet of life, carve out guiding principles for your life that align with the essence. Then, live a life that is both simple and splendid. Let us understand this with an example.

Imagine you face a dilemma—choosing between preserving your relationships or safeguarding your finances. If you understand the essence of relationships, the essence of love, you will formulate life principles that prioritize dedicating quality time to your family, communicating with love, embracing their imperfections, nurturing their strengths, supporting them in challenging times, expressing gratitude for their contributions, pardoning their mistakes, and seeking their forgiveness when you falter. You will integrate these principles into your life and act accordingly, even if it means incurring financial setbacks. Understanding the essence of relationships equips you to navigate through financial losses with readiness.

Let's delve deeper with another example. Imagine you contemplate doing something ethically wrong. If you have understood the essence of karma, then you would establish principles such as never providing false excuses to avoid responsibilities, refraining from aggressive or deceitful actions, steering clear of blaming or complaining about others, being dedicated to your duties, joyfully completing all tasks, and participating in selfless service whenever possible.

In this way, understand the essence of each facet of life, whether social, personal, financial, mental, spiritual, or health-related. After grasping the essence, establish principles that resonate with the essence and steadfastly abide by them.

How to work on the essence hidden in the answers?

This book provides answers that are grounded in the essence of life. When making choices about education, work, business, success, finances, marriage, relationships, health, or the spiritual truth, keep reflecting on your guiding principles in these facets of your life.

By uncompromisingly adhering to principles rooted in life's essence, you will remain equanimous even in the face of setbacks. You will live in alignment with the essence by upholding the principles of your life.

How to benefit from this book

This book is divided into two parts.

1. Part I comprises some common questions related to worldly life. The answers to these questions dispel our ignorance and stupor and lead to an awakening in various facets of life. These answers inspire us to chart out the guiding principles that align with the essence of life.
2. Part II consists of questions on the spiritual facet of life that can inspire seekers in their spiritual pursuit to accelerate their spiritual progress.

The book addresses the challenges of four different age groups – students, the youth, people concerned with worldly affairs, and spiritual seekers. Symbolic images are used to identify the target readers for each question.

 Student

 Youth

 People concerned with worldly affairs

 Spiritual Seekers

If you are confounded by questions relating to worldly life, you can begin reading Part I. But if you are on a spiritual quest, you can directly start with Part II to seek answers to your questions and define the principles for your life based on the essence of spirituality.

PART I

Annihilation of the Mind While Dealing in the World

1
The Essence of Three Things

 When you are troubled by any thought, if you become vigilant, doubt the authenticity of the thought, and introspect its reality, the thought will subside.

Question: In an attempt to please people, I find it difficult to say "No" to them when I have to. Additionally, when my effort to try and align with them goes unappreciated, I feel disappointed. How should I deal with such situations?

Answer: First and foremost, clearly communicate your life's purpose to them. In a loving yet straightforward manner, inform them about what you won't devote your time to. This will help you shape your image in their mind just as you desire.

Gradually, they will realize which areas hold no interest for you. However, this can happen only when you decide the course of your life. Then, no matter how insistently they urge you to compromise on your choices and align with them, you will not fall prey to them and will politely decline. Your steadfast determination will shield you from their unsolicited demands.

For instance, if you are not interested in watching movies or consider it a waste of your time, and your friend insists on your company, you can politely tell them, "Sorry, I won't be able to make it for the movie. I need to finish some important tasks. Instead, you can take along another friend with the same interest." Your friend might be a bit upset initially, but they won't insist you join for a movie next time.

During this situation, you might feel distressed about having displeased your friend by denying them your company. To deal with this distress, you need to be aware of three important aspects:

1. **The present moment:** Feel your internal state in the present moment. When you get caught up in the dilemma, your thoughts can hijack your ability to discern and make the right choice. If your mind is running its mischief, immediately stop it. Only when your mind is calm and you are available in the present moment can you start solving the apparent problem.

2. **The outcome of your past choices:** Watch the present situation as an outcome of your past choices. Contemplate how the choices you've made in your past could be affecting your present life and what changes you need to bring about in your choices.

3. **The power of your prayer:** Sometimes, some of our thoughts from the past can cause confusion and conflict in the present. At such times, strengthen your prayers by visualizing how you want a particular scene to unfold in the future.

By implementing these three things in your daily life, you will experience a balance within yourself and won't get disturbed by others' demands.

> **Essence:** If someone insistently urges an inappropriate demand, politely decline and reinforce your prayers. This is a suitable step towards a bright future.

2
The Essence of the Utility of Things

 *True development can happen only when you use everything in this world as a ladder for spiritual growth, as a means to experience and express the ultimate truth.*

Question: It is said that nothing in the world is useless. So then, how can a rat, for example, be useful?

Answer: Actually, whether a thing is useful or useless entirely depends on our perspective. However, if we look deeper, we will find that useful things gain importance just because some things seem useless. In that sense, the seemingly useless things also prove to be useful.

Honesty is valued because of dishonest people. Beauty is admired in the backdrop of ugliness. Sweetness is favored due to bitter things. When you come to know that everything has a role to play in this world and has its own purpose, you only need to find the evidence to support this fact. Apply this formula to everything and evaluate how it is useful.

For example, if you feel the other person is doing something wrong, contemplate how their behavior is useful to you. By doing something wrong, they warn you against not committing the same mistake. In this way, contemplate the usefulness of each and everything you dislike, and nothing will seem useless to you. Everything in this world will become useful to you. For instance, if you dislike bitter gourd, contemplate how it will improve your health.

Let's consider the example you mentioned. You may find a rat useless, but let's contemplate how it is useful. In Hindu mythology, the rat is believed to be the vehicle of Lord Ganesha. It serves as a reminder of Lord Ganesha. In the medical field, rats have been used as the research subject in laboratories for inventing numerous life-saving drugs. Hence, even scientists have acknowledged their importance. Their sacrifices have paved the way for breakthroughs in developing treatments for a wide range of diseases, from neurological disorders to cardiovascular conditions, and saved the lives of many people. If we contemplate, we will find the evidence.

Once, a rat entered a person's house. He tried hard to catch it. He laid a trap, set a noose, and placed poisoned food items to kill it. However, the rat continued to enjoy its stay. Then, the person's family cleaned the entire house to remove it. After cleaning, they thought of painting the house. Once the house was painted, the rat finally left the house.

Imagine, if it had left earlier, would the family have cleaned and painted the house? Look at what the rat became instrumental for.

In the olden days in India, when a prospective bride's family would visit a prospective groom's family, they would enquire, "Do you have rats in your house?" The question may sound simple, but its answer held a significant clue. If the groom's family said, "Yes, rats keep visiting the house on and off," it meant there was no shortage of food, the family was well-off, and their daughter could live comfortably in that house. The presence of rats was like an assurance of the girl's well-being in her prospective home. Isn't that incredible?

From a scientific angle, rats are an integral part of our ecological cycle, the food chain. They serve as the food source for some animals, and they, too, in turn, feed on some animals. Even if a single creature is taken out of this food chain, it will disrupt the ecological balance in the world. Thus, each and every creature is essential in sustaining the ecological balance. Hence, nothing is useless in this world; everything has a role to play, and everything is complete in itself.

Essence: Rather than seeing things with a limited perspective, learn to broaden your outlook. Everything on Earth is useful and interdependent on each other for their co-existence.

3
The Essence of the Cause of Lies

 *It takes many more lies to conceal one lie, so beware of the first lie. Do not invite an anaconda by avoiding an ant.*

Question: How can we trust someone who lies?

Answer: Firstly, understand that if someone is lying, there must be a reason. No one lies without a reason. So, instead of judging and drawing conclusions, try to find the reason behind their lies.

For instance, if someone lies out of fear or temptation, it could be their habitual behavior. However, the moment we realize that they have lied to us, we start perceiving them negatively and brand them as swindlers, deceptive, and unworthy of trust instead of finding the reason behind their lies.

By creating such stories and narratives, we knowingly or unknowingly judge them. We should always refrain from being judgmental and focus on all the facts. Instead of fabricating stories, try to reason why the other person might lie. Are they afraid of you? Do they want to safeguard their image? Or are they trying to shirk their responsibilities?

Your presence conveys the state of your mind to others. If you draw assumptions, think negatively, and lack trust, it can inadvertently aggravate dishonesty in others. Hence, it is crucial to remain aware, always keep your mind clean, and think positively for others. As your level of awareness rises, your presence also changes for the better.

While interacting with people, your presence should be such that the other person feels encouraged to express themselves openly. This can happen only when they trust that you will never judge them and can comprehend their point of view.

For this, you must behave with them in a straightforward manner. Whenever you meet them, converse in a way that makes them feel fearless. They should never fear that you will exploit their words to your benefit or make fun of them. Your communication should assure them that they need not lie to you and that it is safe for them to tell the truth in your presence.

If they lie out of temptation or some of their personality traits, your pure presence and simple behavior can make them realize that lying is unnecessary, and it can degrade them to a lower level of awareness.

To prevent the other person from lying, you must also develop the habit of telling the truth. Then, you will realize that by speaking and listening to the truth, your level of awareness rises, purifying your mind. Then your behavior becomes simple and straightforward, eliminating the need for any external facades.

For example, a person used to earn ten thousand rupees a month. Some of his friends always used to boast about their salaries in front of him. When asked by one of them, he said he earned twenty thousand a month. He told another friend that his salary was fifteen thousand. However, he told his parents his actual salary.

One day, both his friends visited his house, and their topic of conversation shifted to their jobs and salaries in front of his father. Now, he panicked that his lie would be exposed if they started discussing his salary in front of his father. Just imagine, had he told everyone his true salary, he would not have panicked.

When you are firmly convinced about being truthful, you can convey its importance to others, too. Sharing your experiences in this regard with them can awaken their conscience, and they, too, will bring about change in their behavior. For this to happen, it is essential to win other people's trust instead of judging them. Demonstrate ideal behavior and practical examples before them.

> **Essence:** Your simple and straightforward behavior, pure intention, love, and trust in others gives them an opportunity to speak openly and honestly. This, in turn, also becomes a reason for divine qualities to manifest through you. Your pure, non-judgmental presence will become a catalyst for change.

4
The Essence of Preparing a Backup for Life

 *You cannot prevent what is already happening, but whether to view it from a positive or negative perspective, the choice is certainly yours.*

Question: I often need to lie and deceive at my college to make time to work for a noble cause. But I want my life to be simple and straightforward, doing what I really love. What should be my prayer in such a situation?

Answer: The prayer should be, "At present, I need to resort to deceit to uphold the truth. However, I wish everything comes into my life without guile or deceit."

Every situation that arises in your life is the result of your prayers. A negative situation indicates that you have not clearly defined the backup for your life. To offer an effective prayer with proper words and feelings, you need to be clear about what you wish to manifest in your life.

As part of the backup for your life, you need to give clear inputs to the universe for every facet of your life. In those areas where you are facing problems, you need to sow the seeds of faith, offer prayers, and clearly indicate to the universe how you want to live your life and what kind of people you would like around you. From time to time, verify that your backup is absolutely clear by ensuring that you are not giving confusing inputs to the universe by performing conflicting prayers that cancel one another.

The universe is constantly serving you in abundance on the platter of life. It is up to you to choose what you wish to experience in your life. Don't get caught up with too many things at once. Instead, focus on what you want in the present. Otherwise, people often don't realize the importance of contemplating every aspect, every dimension, every relationship, and every event of their life to lead a fulfilling life.

Different incidents keep happening in life. If your backup is clear, your endeavors get smoothly completed. Without a backup, you experience hurdles on the path and feel discomfort in every task you undertake.

Look at problems in your life with the belief that they are part of the divine plan that will eventually unfold beautifully in the future. You will receive evidence for this, which will reinforce your faith in turn. Hence, when faced with problems, don't let your faith falter by raising doubts, and don't disrupt your backup.

Always tell yourself in clear words, "What do I really want? What do I aspire for?" Write it down clearly. Although others may have different opinions, you must be clear about the kind of life you wish to live. Such contemplation gives shape to the blueprint of the life you wish to live – a backup that evolves into a mature life.

The following aspects encompass a truly mature way of life.

1. **Physical maturity:** It comprises learning proper etiquette and behavior for how to present yourself and deal with others, how to conduct yourself, how to dress appropriately,

and so on. It also includes the aspect of physical discipline with considerations for the right food intake, exercises, and maintenance of your surroundings.

2. **Mental maturity:** This aspect determines whether you make impulsive decisions based on short-term benefits or endure minor difficulties today, considering long-term benefits. Aspects of how you cope with your emotions and leverage them to your benefit also comprise mental maturity.

3. **Financial maturity:** This comprises learning to balance your expenses and savings to strengthen your financial backup.

4. **Social maturity:** This aspect defines your ability to nurture harmony at home and the workplace, fostering a collaborative and progressive social environment around you.

5. **Spiritual maturity:** This aspect helps you regard your entire life holistically and prepare a backup that never wavers. In this manner, you firmly resolve to attain the ultimate goal of your life. Then, no matter what illusory truths like falsehoods, misconceptions, or adverse circumstances you encounter, if your backup is clear, you are bound to achieve your goal. Not only that, but with a clear backup, you will also encounter such people who will guide and support you to progress further.

Deeply contemplate the facets of your life where you feel troubled. It could be about being stuck in traffic, when you are in the kitchen, when you are with people or alone, when you hear the phone ring, when you experience body pain, when you feel hot or cold, when you can't find a parking slot, when people misbehave with you, when you recall hurtful memories, when you worry about the future, when someone surpasses you, when someone's outfit is better than yours, and so on. In all these areas, your backup should be such that these aspects become a cause for your happiness, not distress.

Whenever you encounter negativity in life, turn it into an opportunity to update your backup. In this way, your backup will become more robust, boosting your confidence day by day. Then you will always be happy, and everything will seem possible for you. Moreover, the faith cultivated within you will keep you stable through different situations. Then, no matter what scenes, incidents, situations, people, or problems you encounter, you will face them by staying happy and balanced.

Having such a life, you will always thank the Almighty from dawn to dusk every day, "What a wonderful life I have, where every day is a blessing!"

> **Essence:** To prepare a proper backup, you must develop the right understanding of your life and clarity about your goals and actions. Also, ensure that your prayers and efforts are aligned with your chosen goals.

5
The Essence of Inner Beauty

 *The way to live a happy and contented life is to be in attunement with pure consciousness, the Source within, and allow actions to emerge from inner guidance.*

Question: Since childhood, I have been very fond of wearing different types of clothes and doing makeup. However, from time to time, I wonder, "Is this desire right or not? Do I need to let go of this desire?"

Answer: More than your clothes and makeup, your contemplation is important: Whether you are aligned with the Source within and in harmony with the world outside, whether you have become pure and free of deceit. Clothes do have their own importance. They are meant to protect our bodies in different weather conditions and are worn according to the necessity and environment. Rise above the need to flaunt clothes as your identity and check whether your inner character has become truly refined and mature. People should know you by your accomplishments, not your appearance.

Your pursuit of physical beauty is immaterial. Whether you become free from your desire to wear different types of clothes doesn't really matter because desires incessantly arise and subside every moment. Instead of focusing on the desires that entangle you, examine whether you feel a sense of oneness with the world. If you are experiencing conflict or confusion within and continue to portray yourself as someone who you really aren't in the outside world, pray to God, "Please help me get out of this state as soon as possible. Let Thy will be mine." Then, don't worry about the outcome of the prayer. Enjoy the free flow of life.

Essence: Raising our level of consciousness is more important than our physical appearance or clothing. Our aim should be to live a life of integrity – our feelings, thoughts, speech, and actions should be in alignment. Let our contemplation and actions steer us in this direction.

6
The Essence of Undesirable Incidents

Until you are convinced that people are just meant to be exactly as they are, you will keep disliking them and hurting yourself.

Question: When things don't happen as I would like, how can I say, "Let Thy will be my will"? For instance, if my brother snatches the TV remote from my hand and switches to a channel I dislike, how can I apply the above statement?

Answer: "Thy will is my will" is not being addressed to any individual; it is a sentiment towards God's will.

When your brother switches to a channel you dislike, you do not have to say this to him but to God. It helps you accept the situation, letting go of your resistance. Resisting the situation gives rise to conflicts within. Otherwise, problems get resolved easily. Therefore, whenever you encounter an undesirable incident, this mantra is very effective. It not only helps you accept any situation but also enables you to see the underlying invisible meaning of the incident.

When your brother changes the channel, and you don't think or feel positive, you will either argue with him or silently complain and sulk. However, if you quickly remember, "Thy will is my will," you will calmly think, "Oh! He has changed my favorite channel; what should I do now?" It is possible that you may remember a long pending task and decide to do it instead of watching TV. Or you may try to lovingly convince your brother to switch back to your favorite channel. You don't know what kind of response will emerge from within you.

If you are able to accept the incident, you will respond positively and feel happy. If you are not, your mind will keep complaining and be unhappy: "Why did my brother do this? He shouldn't have done it. How dare he? My brother is dim-witted. He always does this to me," and so on.

When you tell God, "Thy will is my will," you are convinced that your brother did precisely what was meant to happen as per the divine will, whether it aligns with your desires or not. This does not mean that you passively sit and watch whatever is happening. Instead, with a feeling of acceptance, contemplate how God wants you to respond to the situation.

With this understanding, learn to look at every incident as it is. There is no need to complain or blame anyone. If you think, "My brother is dim-witted," doubt your own sanity: "Do you love your preferred channel more than your brother?"

When your brother switched to his channel, a channel of complaints, dislike, and resistance started streaming within you. Instead, a channel of introspection should start streaming within you: "Why is this incident necessary in my life? What hidden aspects of my nature are being brought to light through this incident that are hindering my peace and growth?"

Every minutest incident can become instrumental for your introspection. Observe how your mind chatters during an incident. What does it want? In this manner, if you examine your thoughts, introspect them, and uncover your underlying unnecessary desires, you will wonder, "My brother started the right channel at the right time. I was unnecessarily getting worked up. This incident has helped me reflect and bring to light what was indeed necessary for my growth."

Believe it; every incident in life can help you progress towards your highest evolved version. You may not apparently realize from the outside how the seemingly negative incident is actually serving your needs or helping you progress. You must contemplate deeply and thoroughly to uncover the lessons hidden within the incident.

In this scene, God arranged to take away the TV remote from your hands and switch to the channel you dislike by your brother so that the right channel of understanding runs within you. You can use this incident as a medium to gain insight into your mind and to revel in the bliss of self-discovery.

> **Essence:** Your every prayer instills faith in God, provides a perspective to perceive incidents, and enhances the feeling of acceptance in your mind. This allows you to view incidents with poise and maturity.

7
The Essence of Understanding Nature's Hints

 *Nature has everything in abundance for everyone: Love, joy, peace, harmony in relationships, time, health, prosperity, virtues, supreme wisdom, and so forth. Those who are ever grateful for these blessings experience abundance in all facets of their lives.*

Question: How can I identify what I really want to achieve in life? Please guide me.

Answer: To know what you truly want in life, first calm your mind and write down what you desire. Writing down your desires often leads you to the answers. The answer to "What do I want?" emerges from within. But you cannot hear this inner voice unless your mind is still.

Additionally, try to grasp the hints emanating from your surroundings. Situations in life provide you with clues about what you really want, the direction your life is heading, and the direction you should take.

For instance, if you frequently encounter people involved in the service of society while managing their careers, you may also be encouraged to engage in social service. Similarly, if you meet people who focus on their health, it could indicate your wish to attain good health.

To understand these indications, try to assess what every place, incident, or person is conveying. They indicate what you really want.

Many times, you are taught the right thing by showing an exactly opposite scene. For instance, you visit a house full of abundance, prosperity, and affluent people, but there is discord among the family members. It makes you think, "The most essential thing in life is harmony in the family. Even if other things are lacking, I want a life filled with happiness and peace."

This prayer will help you dwell in the present and work efficiently. People will wonder how you could achieve what most others couldn't. Although it may seem difficult in the beginning, with your diligence, everything will resolve naturally, leading you in the right direction.

Therefore, live with awareness and keep noting whatever indications are becoming clear to you. This will help you find the path that will eventually lead you to what you really want.

> **Essence:** When you introspect events with a calm mind and awareness, you will discover what you truly want in life.

8
The Essence of Being Aware Every Moment

 *The mind always prefers to do things the old way because it can afford to be less aware while walking the beaten path. Therefore, work hard on new tasks or perform familiar tasks in new ways to raise your awareness.*

Question: How can I stay 100% aware every moment, with every task?

Answer: You might have seen the domino formation, where pushing a small initial tile triggers a chain reaction, knocking over larger and larger tiles, continuing till the end. Similarly, even a herculean task can be accomplished by starting with a small task.

If someone has been living without much awareness for years and wishes to wake up to a 100% aware life in a day, it is not possible. Instead, they should focus on identifying the smallest tile that can be knocked to cause the domino fall. In other words, identify and start with small tasks that can be done with 100% awareness. Every day, try to identify tasks that can be easily done consciously. Aspire to reach 100% but start with a small goal: "I want to raise my level of awareness to 20% this year." Otherwise, you may become disappointed if you wish to achieve 100% awareness at the first step itself.

When you complete twenty small tasks out of a hundred with full awareness in a day, it will prepare you for your next milestone of knocking the next bigger tile, i.e., the 2-inch tile will cause the next 4-inch tile to fall. If you try to knock down the mountain in the first step itself, it will seem impossible. But with the example of the domino effect, you understood how a two-inch tile causes a four-inch tile to fall, which in turn causes the next eight-inch tile to fall.

Whatever be the result you wish to achieve in the future, prepare for it by taking small steps. Set small goals and stick to them. When you carefully observe these small goals and tasks, you will clearly observe that you performed these 20% tasks with complete awareness and the remaining 80% tasks were completed unconsciously. This will make you aware of your unawareness, and you will notice when you were unaware throughout the day. This will propel you faster toward your goal. You will soon progress from 20% to 40%, then 80%, and eventually attain 100% awareness.

Essence: In the beginning, take small steps deliberately and complete them with awareness. This will boost your confidence, making you believe "I can do it!" When you will monitor your actions, you will clearly see what actions are performed with and without awareness. This awareness of your non-awareness will make you aware of your goals and accelerate your efforts toward achieving them. This way, you can attain 100% awareness.

9
The Essence of Solving Any Problem

 *Through experiences, you come to know the truth that there is no need to be unhappy; you can always choose to be happy. This choice leads to rapid resolution of problems.*

Question: What is the mindset of those who engage in negative incidents and crimes in society? We hear about grave and gruesome crimes committed during times of war and through terrorism. Why do the perpetrators commit such crimes, and what is the solution to this problem?

Answer: Every incident, whether good or bad, has two aspects. One is the visible aspect, which has already manifested and the other is the invisible aspect that is yet to manifest. When we look at it from a bird's eye view, everything is happening according to the divine will. The visible aspect is the first part of the divine will while the invisible aspect is the second part of the divine will.

Let us understand this with an example. There was a time when the entire world was going through severe strife and turmoil due to the devastating consequences of World War II. People were extremely depressed by the loss of human life and property and fed up with the fallout of the war. Then, to prevent another world war, the leaders of all countries came together and formed the United Nations Organization. Through the medium of the UNO, they could amicably resolve issues between nations through dialogue and negotiation and take steps to prevent the proliferation of conflicts. However, for this situation to arise, the entire world had to first endure the consequences of war. Thus, some events shake up the entire world. Then, these events become the reason for a new creation.

Let us understand this with a few more examples. Jesus was crucified; severe pain was inflicted to his body. Socrates was poisoned to death. However, when perceived today, the gruesome end that their bodies were subjected to has not been in vain. Those incidents, which were the first part of the divine will, became instrumental for the world to recognize the power of faith and forgiveness, to uplift the value of wisdom. This is the second part of the divine will. The first part of the incident led to the second part, which was invisible at first.

Similarly, when a crime or any other negative incident occurs, it raises people's sensitivity and gives momentum to the resolution of long pending cases in fast-track courts to fulfill people's growing demand to punish the guilty at the earliest. Subsequently, new laws come into place to safeguard the victims and prosecute the guilty. However, for this to happen, some people become victims and suffer the adverse consequences of the incidents, which in turn leads to positive changes that help the world.

However, when such negative incidents occur, people cannot comprehend the whole picture, part of which is invisible at that time. Hence, they focus on the first part of the incident and keep lamenting, "Nothing good is happening in the world." As they firmly believe in the partial truth, they get more evidence for that, and their belief is reinforced.

In reality, our fears, victim mindset, and hidden insecurities attract adverse incidents into our lives. Once we understand this hidden secret, we will strive to rise above our fears, feelings of insecurity, and negative mindset. If we think with an open mind, we will realize that solutions to every major global problem are being sought through a combination of ideas from people worldwide.

To change anything, it is important to first bring about a change at the level of thoughts; prayer serves as a medium to do that. When we pray, we sow seeds of positive change in our thoughts because everything gets created first on the mental plane and later manifests on the physical plane. Events that happen around us help garner the thoughts that are necessary for new creations.

Hence, instead of feeling sad and regretting over negative events, it is more helpful to change our thoughts and focus our faith not on the events but on positive solutions. With this approach, we will find that such incidents serve to bring forth solutions to unresolved issues; without this approach, we continue to suffer for years. Therefore, instead of labeling the events as good or bad, we should sow seeds of positivity through prayers.

The power of our prayers will work through the universe, and everyone will seek solutions at their own level. Scientists will develop devices that will be useful to people during times of crisis. Teachers will contemplate how to teach children creatively and playfully. Lawyers will ponder the laws that could be enacted to eliminate crime rather than criminals.

Our prayers will be instrumental in bringing about such new changes. Therefore, let us look at incidents without labels and keep faith in bringing forth a better future.

Essence: We should view incidents with an open mind, make efforts, and offer prayer to transcend their negative impacts. We must always have faith that if something is being destroyed, something new is bound to be created, which will bring happiness and progress on the global stage.

10
The Essence of Watch, Wait with Wonder

 *"Watch, Wait with Wonder" are not just words; they hold incredible power that can help stop the needless somersaults of the mind in the past and the future by teaching us the art of living in the present moment.*

Question: In "Watch, Wait with Wonder," the waiting period sometimes feels endless. When I witness wonders, waiting becomes easier. However, there are instances when, despite experiencing marvels, troubles do not diminish. What can be done in such situations?

Answer: Every problem in life is orchestrated by nature as a result of various people's prayers.

Often, we see in movies that the protagonist, despite being a good-hearted person, is inflicted with continuous troubles and obstacles by the villain. However, they remain steadfast in their actions and ultimately achieve the desired outcome.

The contrasting desires of the protagonist and the villain give rise to various incidents in the film. However, most of the time, the film ends on a positive note. If we assume ourselves to be the main character and watch the incidents with the understanding of "Watch,

Wait with Wonder," we realize that the main character need not have been so distressed; they could have endured the period with the understanding of "Watch, Wait with Wonder."

Similarly, enjoy the game of life like you would have enjoyed the movie. You do not know where the game of life will lead you, what will unfold from the current challenges, and whether it will give rise to conflicts or happiness. Everything is unknown. Hence, observe what is happening now and what will happen later with a sense of wonder.

When you get lost in thoughts, ask yourself, "From which thought did this thought arise? What was the preceding thought?" By doing this, you reach the point from where your attention was diverted. Once you start enjoying this process, you will also witness wonders. Then, these things will become the cause of your joy, not distress. By contemplating this way, you will not feel bored even during the waiting time. Until the complete mystery of a scene is revealed, keep watching every incident with wonder, "Now that this has come, let's see what will happen next."

In every event, understand that the scene has been created as the outcome of everyone's prayers. Now, witness with wonder how this gets resolved. For instance, some activity that was stuck, suddenly gets resolved through some news, a phone call, or the completion of a small task. A moment ago, you were unaware of it, and the next moment, the desired result manifested. Such revelations can happen at any moment. Learn to witness them with wonder and childlike curiosity.

Be in harmony with nature, in alignment with God, until you witness the moment of wonder. Your internal state indicates whether you are in harmony or not. If you are out of alignment, restore it by practicing *Sadhana*, spiritual practice, by performing meditation, offering prayer, or using positive self-affirmations. Everything in this world is happening based on this principle. Even the resolution to a significant problem depends on how aligned you are with God. Otherwise, people live in a dual mindset. On the one hand, they say, "We want to resolve the problem," on the other hand, they wish, "Let the problem remain unresolved, as it benefits us." As a result, the problem remains unresolved.

Your alignment with God should be such that even the slightest disturbance in that harmony will make you practice Sadhana to restore the alignment. This realignment will make you feel positive, causing the resolution of all problems at hand. If you believe in the phrase, **"Nature is serving everything in accordance with your divine plan**," then despite all the problems, you will live life happily with wonder. Then gradually, you will start deducing the secret of all forthcoming events and challenges in your life.

As you will understand the secret, you will be amazed and exclaim, "Oh, this was supposed to be resolved like this!" In this way, every moment can become incredibly beautiful, but the mind does not readily accept this. Hence, practice Sadhana to get the mind to accept it. Everything else will then happen naturally. With this understanding, when solutions manifest, you will surely enjoy them. However, you can even enjoy it during the waiting period, so that it will not be in vain.

If you consider karma itself as the fruit, you can rejoice in everything. Then, you will enjoy the beautiful process of getting distracted and then regaining the state of harmony with the practice of Sadhana. In this way, life will become a source of pure bliss.

Essence: When you observe even the smallest event with wonder, you can see it in its entirety and rejoice. Otherwise, you get stuck in it. Therefore, continue to practice Sadhana to be aligned with nature in every situation so that you will not feel confused during that period and the problem will be resolved smoothly.

11
The Essence of Happiness and Faith

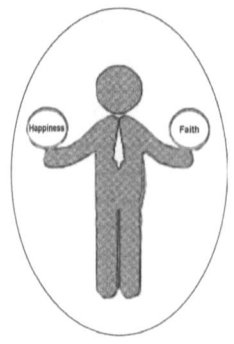

The habit of consciously bringing forth thoughts of happiness is invaluable. It turns you into a powerful magnet, attracting all those things in the universe essential for achieving your goal.

Question: Can I attain everything in life by just being happy?

Answer: This question has two parts that complement each other.

When you are happy, you become a magnet that attracts whatever you desire in your life, and as a result, you continue to dwell in the same state of happiness. Thus, happiness makes you a magnet, and being a magnet begets even more happiness, enabling your divine plan to manifest.

Most people tend to believe, "I can be happy only if I get that particular thing or if that specific desired incident happens." Then, they remain sad during the waiting period. However, if you dwell in a feeling of happiness with faith, whatever you desire will be attracted in your life automatically.

God desires to experience happiness through the medium of various bodies, without any discrimination based on gender, education, abilities, or the lack of it. The entire arrangement has been made for that purpose, and its first condition is happiness. If you remain happy, things that are according to your divine plan will manifest in your life.

After praying for what you desire, when you remain happy, you can experience the same joy right now that you would experience when your prayers are fulfilled in the future. Your happiness is a declaration of your unshakeable faith: **"I have full faith that my prayer will be answered."**

Each person may have a different way of expressing their happiness. Some may laugh, while others may not. But what matters is that they are genuinely happy within; their essential feeling of happiness prepares them for the ultimate freedom. The happiness experienced after attaining this freedom is beyond everyday happiness. Hence, it is referred to as "*Sat Chit Anand*," unconditional bliss, supreme joy, everlasting happiness.

> **Essence:** When you remain happy, you indirectly fulfill the will of God. Hence, it is important to be happy. This turns you into a magnet that automatically attracts all things that are part of your divine plan into your life.

12
The Essence of Need and Want

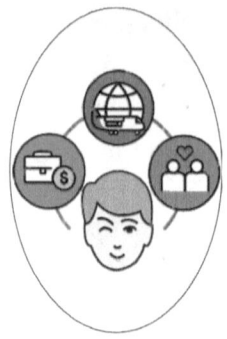

 *Whenever you plan to buy something, ask yourself, "Is this my need or want?"*

Question: What is the difference between needs and wants?

Answer: Needs and wants can vary from one person to another. Something that is a necessity for one person could be a mere want or an extravagance for another. For example, a car may be a necessity for a businessman, but it may just be a status symbol or an extravagant spend for someone else.

When you tend to feel emotionally attached to something, you may end up buying it even if it is not your necessity. As long as such an attachment does not harm you or anyone else, there is no harm in purchasing that thing. However, if it causes harm to others, you will have to bear the consequences of those harmful actions. Let us understand this with an example.

If you use your credit card to pay for some medical emergency, it is undoubtedly a necessity; you must fulfill it. However, if you don't have enough money in your bank account and still swipe your credit card for non-essential shopping and later struggle to repay your credit card bills and the interest thereon, it is surely a needless want. Had you questioned yourself beforehand with awareness, "Is this a need or a want?" you could have avoided this loss. Therefore, before proceeding with anything, make it a habit to ask yourself, "Is this a need or a want?" and then take the next step.

Prioritize fulfilling necessities even if you have to endure some difficulty in acquiring them. However, certainly, avoid pursuing things that you can do without; they are wants.

Reflect on your desires and discern whether they are needs or wants. This will enhance your understanding and alertness and help you make the right decisions.

> **Essence:** Before any task, mindfully ask yourself, "Is this really a need or just a want? Will it create any unnecessary trouble?" Only then should you proceed further with the task.

13
The Essence of Sad Incidents

 Regardless of the ups and downs life presents, maintain your inner equanimity. This is the path to a truly free and stabilized life.

Question: How do we handle ourselves during sad incidents?

Answer: Do you mean to say that you do not understand the right thing to do during sorrowful situations? To navigate such circumstances effectively, you need to prepare yourself beforehand. Proactively decide what you should and shouldn't do during such situations. For example, be mindful of your thoughts and feelings and affirm, "I genuinely love myself, so I will vigilantly observe what triggers sadness within me." When faced with such situations, analyze your responses and assess how you tend to get trapped, leading to self-resentment.

When you maintain your inner peace and balance yourself, everything else will naturally fall into place. For this, you need to prepare yourself proactively. Make a list of five things you will do to feel happy and positive when faced with a situation that evokes sadness.

Once you are done with your proactive preparation, put it into practice. Attentively observe which incidents trigger sadness or make you feel trapped or constricted. Remind yourself, "Regardless of the circumstances or the negative incidents that occur, I will maintain my inner peace and joy." Then, try to stay steadfast during real-time situations and assess your progress throughout the day. Those who genuinely love themselves will not get entangled in such events; they will remain steadfast regardless of external circumstances. This will help reduce the unrest within you, enabling you to maintain inner peace successfully.

Essence: Minimize inner turmoil through proactive preparation. Gradually learn to be steadfast in all situations. By doing so, you will learn to maintain the same love, joy, and self-belief, both internally and externally.

14
The Essence of the Quality of Sleep

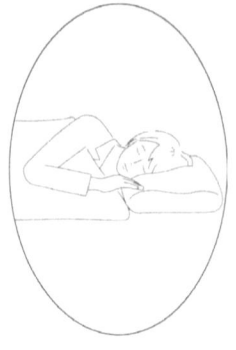

 *Take rest ahead of exhaustion and commence work before laziness sets in.*

Question: How can I improve the quality of my sleep so that my daytime productivity remains unaffected by inadequate sleep?

Answer: The quality of your nighttime sleep is influenced by how you spend your day. If your body is experiencing illness or distress, it can negatively affect your sleep. To enhance the quality of your nighttime sleep, you must improve the quality of your daytime activities.

To achieve this, you need to inculcate discipline into your daily routine, starting with waking up early in the morning. This will enable you to complete all your activities smoothly and on time.

If you face interruptions or undesirable situations during the day, first accept them with ease and a composed attitude. Life comes with challenges, but embracing them with grace empowers you to navigate every small or big problem with ease.

For example, if your body is unwell, it can disturb your sleep. In such a situation, first accept it. Then, incorporate proper diet, medicine, and sufficient rest in your daily routine. Reading or listening to some good literature can support in speedy recovery and also enable you to sleep well.

If your tasks remain incomplete, you often go to bed with a sense of incompleteness in your mind. This can lead to seeing those tasks in your dreams, potentially affecting the quality of your sleep.

Hence, the best approach is to handle a workload that you can comfortably manage. If there is an excessive workload, consider creating a priority list. Complete the most important tasks first and leave the less urgent ones for the following day. However, refrain from carrying work-related stress to bed at night. Instead, engage in a relaxed visualization of how your tasks will be completed the following day. When your visualization is clear and relaxed, nature often assists you in its successful execution.

Our body naturally acquires the sleep it needs. There is no need to worry about the duration of the sleep. Otherwise, many people believe that "Eight hours of sleep is ideal" and judge the quality of their sleep solely by the clock using this benchmark. If they sleep that long, they believe they had a good sleep. Otherwise, they think, "Something is wrong; I didn't sleep well." Don't categorize sleep in this manner. Everyone is unique, with distinct lifestyles, daily routines, and challenges. So, how can the duration of sleep be the same for all?

Some people feel refreshed even after a short nap, while others find solace in meditation. Some feel completely refreshed after a six-hour sleep, while others might struggle with daytime drowsiness despite having slept for eight hours.

How soon a mobile phone gets charged depends on its battery and charger. With a good battery, the right charger, and sufficient power input, the phone gets charged quickly. Otherwise, even an extended period of charging may not be effective without these things. Similarly, when your health and mental well-being are in good condition, even a short duration of sleep can keep you energized and revitalized.

If you still want to make some last-minute efforts before bedtime, regardless of how your day unfolded, ensure to keep your sleeping space clean, comfortable, and well-ventilated. Take a moment to sit comfortably on your bed and express gratitude to it. Then, take a few deep breaths and repeat some positive affirmations.

Tailor your affirmations to suit your current needs. For example, if you are studying, focus on affirmations related to studies; if you have health issues, repeat affirmations related to health. Customize your affirmations to align with the specific facets of your life that you are dealing with. You can even consider recording them and listening for reinforcement.

Before going to bed, envision how you would like to start the next day. Imagine yourself commencing the day with love, joy, and peace. Visualize successfully completing all your tasks in a timely manner throughout the day. Your visualization is a kind of prayer. By doing so, you convey to nature how you want to spend your next day and how your mental state should be throughout the day.

When you drift off to sleep after visualizing pleasant scenes and positive thoughts, it can significantly impact the following day. The thoughts repeated just before sleep are like seeds planted in our subconscious mind, and they undoubtedly bear fruit. Hence, before sleeping, sow positive seeds of self-belief and faith in your subconscious mind to nurture an optimistic outlook for the following day.

Apart from this, repeat the following affirmation:

"I had a wonderful day today, and in tonight's sleep, I am preparing for an amazing day tomorrow. May I receive all the things that are necessary for this to happen. May the knowledge that I need be made available to me."

Essence: The quality of your life significantly impacts your sleep. You must alter your lifestyle if there are disturbances in your night's sleep.

15
The Essence of Livelihood

 *Earning a livelihood is only part of the complete goal of life. Besides earning a livelihood, when you keep the ultimate purpose of life in mind, that constitutes the complete goal.*

Question: How can I determine the right livelihood for myself?

Answer: Whatever type of livelihood you choose, it can prove to be the highest choice, provided you have contemplated why you are pursuing it and its outcome. This contemplation will elevate your awareness.

For instance, if someone considers entering the liquor business, you can easily understand its impact on society. Hence, it is crucial to reflect on the overall implications of any occupation before engaging in it.

On honest reflection, if you realize that your choices will yield positive outcomes, you may proceed in that direction. If you belong to a group of people with higher awareness, you can contemplate collectively with them. Then, decision-making will become easier for you. However, you will also have to fully own up to the consequences of the decisions you make.

Also, check whether your decision is influenced by fear or external pressure. For instance, if you reluctantly agree to a task requested by an elderly family member, contemplate first, gather all relevant information about the task, and strive to eliminate any form of pressure or fear that could impair your decision.

Knowledge plays a crucial role in decision-making. At times, the absence of information can hinder us from making the right decisions because we lack a comprehensive understanding of all the facets involved in the decision, and no guidance is available. When faced with such uncertainty, if you begin with a task and subsequently discover challenges or issues, you can change the direction of that task. For that, you must be clear about the intention behind that task.

If you contemplate all the above aspects, it will be easier to make decisions because you will surely have to engage in some activity to earn your livelihood. Ensure that your choice helps you enhance your purity and attain the ultimate purpose of life. Then your decision will be right.

Question: If I am required to move away from the Guru for the sake of livelihood, how should I make this decision?

Answer: First and foremost, observe whether things come to you effortlessly and naturally. If they are, consider it as a positive indication from nature. Otherwise, many people encounter several hurdles when striving to achieve success or attain certain milestones in life. Even while they ardently pray for success, they may fail because their own prayers are not aligned with their chosen livelihood. However, if you easily get a livelihood that harmonizes with your divine plan, you can surely proceed with benevolent feelings.

For instance, if you get your passport, visa, and finances to relocate abroad smoothly and easily, consider it as a cue from nature to proceed further.

Always remember that wherever you are, maintain your awareness and conscious way of life, learning valuable lessons on the way. Never compromise on your core values.

If you take care of these aspects, rest assured that the Guru's guidance will serve you well. In this digital age, no matter where you are, you can stay connected with the Guru's teachings; this is the highest use of technology.

> **Essence:** Expressing our virtues while performing our duties and progressing toward the highest purpose of life is the real goal of our livelihood.

16
The Essence of Emotions

One doesn't become truly mature by merely aging. True emotional maturity is attained only when one learns the art of witnessing and enduring emotions in the right way, without being influenced by them.

Question: Is being emotional a strength or a weakness?

Answer: Being emotional can be a weakness and also a strength. Let us understand this with an example.

There is a house with four rooms: the room of emotions, the room of discerning power, the room of equanimity, and the room of understanding. The room of understanding holds the key to access the first three rooms.

It can be a weakness if you get stuck in the room of emotions because once you are confined there, you may miss experiencing the other three rooms or have a delayed experience of them. If you are told, "You can enter only one of these four rooms," you would have to make a choice.

In such a situation, you should choose the fourth room of understanding first, where you will understand how to access the other three rooms. This will help you retain your level of awareness, making it easier for you to perceive the wonders of the first three rooms.

Human beings are gifted with emotions to enjoy their short visit to Earth. By experiencing every emotion and emerging from it, we gain inner strength. However, people often get caught up in their emotions and remain unhappy. When they are overwhelmed by their emotions, they cannot think rationally and remain trapped in the sway of their emotions. This significantly weakens their inner strength.

For instance, someone tells a child, "Complete this task, and I will reward you with an ice cream." The child is emotionally attached to the ice cream and completes the task for that sake. However, they remain unaware of the other rooms connected to the experience of completing the task. They remain oblivious to the other benefits they could have achieved by completing the task besides just acquiring the ice cream.

Likewise, many people often get carried away by their emotions and get entangled while helping others without being aware of the boundaries they need to adhere to. It is akin to some psychiatrists and counselors, who try to help the depressed, only to get trapped in their sorrowful emotions in the process of treating them.

This is like burning your hands while trying to extinguish the fire. When you apply the right understanding, your emotional nature can become your strength. When emotions are aided with understanding, you can empathize with others' sorrow. When paired with the power of discernment, you can find solutions to alleviate their sorrow. You can harmonize your understanding and discerning power with equanimity. This way, you will not be inundated by others' sorrow but rather understand yourself with profound self-awareness, thus rendering the highest help to others.

Essence: If you are able to sustain your level of awareness amidst emotions, it becomes your strength. If you are able to maintain this state of higher awareness consistently, you can leverage the power of your discernment and understanding to become the master of your inner strength.

17
The Essence of Freedom from Beliefs

Nature is always ready to provide abundantly, but often, our beliefs hold us back from receiving it properly. Hence, decode the indications from nature with an open mind and live life fearlessly.

Question: Currently, the topic of getting me married is being discussed at home. I fear that my partner's beliefs will also influence my life after marriage. Please guide me in this matter.

Answer: You wish to comprehend certain truths while sitting on the shore of life, but true understanding often requires you to dive deep into the ocean of life experiences. You gain clarity on certain things only after going through some situations. The key is to keep your foundation strong.

Deeply reflect on your present actions and the prayers you are performing based on the wisdom you have received. Do your prayers remain steadfast or falter in antagonistic or challenging situations? How stable is your life at present?

With the introduction of a new family or living situation, there may be new challenges that could potentially lead to distress. Yet, if you have learned how to navigate these situations, you can be assured and confident. If you respond correctly in adverse situations, you will witness the problems getting resolved by themselves.

However, if you approach new situations with a preconceived notion like, "How can harmony be achieved?" or "This seems so difficult," then set these thoughts aside and pray, "May I attain absolute harmony in the forthcoming situation."

Often, thoughts keep churning in our minds, confounding us. At such times, consider jotting them down on paper as a means to gain a clear understanding. You may discard the writing later when it has outlived its purpose.

Moreover, in every incident, cultivate the understanding that whatever be the karma that has brought this distress, I must accept it gracefully. By doing so, you can free yourself from the karmic bondage and further recurrences. All those people or situations with which you share karmic bondages will keep appearing in your life to help you in liberation from this bondage. Thank them from the bottom of your heart.

If someone irritates and overtakes you in the traffic, remind yourself, "This is a karmic bondage that has been settled." Avoid creating a new karmic account of bondage by rebuking them in return. Instead, with this understanding, thank them. You can also seek forgiveness from them mentally. The deeper your understanding and the higher your awareness, the more easily you can seek forgiveness from others.

As your awareness rises, things become easier. Your present preparation will serve you well in this regard. The wisdom you have gained today should be treated like arrows in your quiver, to be used at the right time. Remember that every arrow that you shoot will return to you. Hence, learn to discern which arrows to shoot and which to withhold.

You cannot predetermine every scene and prepare for it. It depends on what unfolds in a scene and how your mind reacts to it. Before responding to a situation, calm down first. Remind yourself, "I have to delay my response." Take a pause to decide on your next course of action. This practice will help you in your further endeavors.

When the mind is in turmoil, instead of adding fuel to the storm by becoming more agitated, exercise patience; the storm will eventually subside. Relationships thrive when there is mutual understanding. In new relationships, you may judge them initially out of habit. However, you can observe them as they are and accept them without making assumptions. For this, you should develop the ability to perceive life as a whole without bias.

When you are aligned internally and externally, people can understand you easily. Conversely, when you put up a different external façade, people may struggle to understand you. For some people, this misalignment persists for many years in some relationships because they are unable to openly express what they truly want. They anticipate that others will understand their needs without explicitly stating them, but this expectation is often unmet. Ambiguity in relationships can lead to distress, while clarity fosters harmonious relationships.

> **Essence:** Do not nurture preconceived beliefs or fears about a new situation before confronting it. Stay open, raise your awareness, and prepare yourself with the highest prayers daily. This will help safeguard you from any sudden dilemmas.

18
The Essence of Divine Occupation

 *Just as iron can be used to cut iron, similarly, whenever negative thoughts arise, and feelings of rejection or resistance emerge in the mind, they need to be countered with positive thoughts.*

Question: I am deeply dissatisfied with my current job. It makes me feel perturbed and sad. I want to dedicate my life to solving social problems. Please guide me on this.

Answer: Let us understand the answer to this question in five steps.

1. The present condition is a preparation for a new creation in the future. The world needs people who can solve problems. There are more problem creators than problem solvers in the world. Most of the people are neither problem creators nor problem solvers. They should be considered problem creators because they do not contribute to the world's progress. They are mere followers in the crowd. The number of solvers must increase to uplift the world, and your intention aligns with this goal.

2. When you find it difficult to accept something, you feel frustrated. At such times, firmly decide and affirm to yourself that problem solvers do not succumb to frustration, and neither should I. Frustration hinders the problem-solving

process, potentially leading to getting entangled in the problems themselves. Hence, earnestly pray for moving from non-acceptance to acceptance.

3. If you currently struggle to accept certain things, consider them as the need of the moment and embrace them. Over time, you will realize their merits. This shift will liberate you from frustration and sorrow, enabling you to actively participate in resolving global issues and becoming a genuine problem solver.

4. Remind yourself, "By liberating myself from this frustration, I will attain my goal." For this, identify those minor issues that you find challenging to accept, that drain your energy and lead to frustration and sorrow. If there is something big, you become aware of it. However, these small, seemingly insignificant things linger in your subconscious mind without your awareness. Take note of them and contemplate them in solitude.

5. If your role is to alleviate the sorrow of others, you must first witness your own sorrow. Be ever prepared without fear because you may find yourself confronted with adverse situations or problems unexpectedly. In such moments, contemplate the wisdom that "Those who witness and comprehend the depth of their own suffering can help others." Lord Buddha fully witnessed and comprehended his own suffering, which led to his liberation from all sorrows, and he, in turn, became instrumental in liberating others from their sufferings. Similarly, prepare yourself so that you can also contribute to the betterment of the world.

Essence: Through purposeful and focused contemplation, eliminate the feeling of rejection and resistance from your mind. Utilize the available time to gain more knowledge and train yourself for the highest livelihood. In the process of solving problems, you are continuously learning. This learning will make you capable of helping others.

19
The Essence of the Highest Programming

 *Our subconscious mind is akin to Aladdin's magic lamp, ever ready to aid us. If we learn to harness it correctly, we can achieve all we aspire to in life.*

Question: How can we harness the powers of our subconscious mind to attain the highest and most fulfilling livelihood?

Answer: It is best to harness the inherent powers of the subconscious mind—a gift bestowed upon us—while staying aligned with our true goal, our ultimate purpose.

Our body is a powerful tool that encompasses the innate power of our subconscious mind that can be used to attain our goals. When you realize who you truly are and recognize the powers of your subconscious mind, you need not lead a life of servitude. With the power of the subconscious mind, you can dispel your false beliefs, and in the process, besides the goals of livelihood, your ultimate purpose on Earth also becomes evident.

To master the powers of the subconscious mind, it must be awakened and activated. You can use techniques like NLP (Neuro-Linguistic Programming), EFT (Emotional Freedom Techniques), hypnosis, and affirmations. While these techniques help raise awareness, their fundamental basis is meditation.

The conscious mind dwells in limiting beliefs, which can pose a hurdle for your intentions to impregnate the subconscious mind. Hence, first, calm and slow down your conscious mind through meditation, allowing your thoughts to penetrate the subconscious mind. As external thoughts reduce, space is created, enabling you to plant your thoughts like seeds in the fertile soil of your subconscious mind. When you firmly believe that you are happy and act accordingly, your mind becomes programmed for that. While it may require initial effort, it becomes second nature over time.

The wrong beliefs held in the subconscious mind can be dismantled through concentration and willpower. When you program your mind with affirmations such as "I can do it. It is possible for me. Using the power of my subconscious mind, I can attract the right things into my life," you will witness corresponding results. This, in turn, will help you conserve the time and energy that you waste on unproductive thoughts that hinder your growth.

To kindle such faith and readiness within, you must embark on the journey of self-awakening through meditation and understanding. You will then eventually see yourself effortlessly achieving what you aspire to.

Therefore, with the right intention and by harnessing the power of your subconscious mind, you can make the best use of the time saved to attain your highest goal. Once you awaken this power within you, take a moment and introspect whether your ego has been kindled in the process. If it has, you might become a slave to the very power you have activated and harnessed.

Often, it has been observed that those who have not progressed on the spiritual facet of their life may acquire this power but become ensnared by their ego and the trap of occult powers. Hence, raising awareness is paramount. Keep observing yourself at every step because no one else can understand you better than yourself. Maintain a vigilant watch over your emotions and thoughts, ensuring you use the acquired power solely for the highest purpose—your progress and that of others.

> **Essence:** Using the power of the subconscious mind is the best way of achieving our livelihood goals or life purpose. However, harnessing the powers of the subconscious mind requires learning through meditation and awareness. Additionally, choosing our purpose with utmost awareness is essential. Once we have diligently prepared in both these aspects, we can effectively use the power of the subconscious mind to make a positive and profound impact.

20

The Essence of the Final Tool

Awareness is the most important tool to successfully tide through the sea of life. By being vigilant and contemplating the incidents happening daily, you can gather and get rid of the burden of thoughts that lie scattered in your life.

Question: How do I identify a permanent solution in an incident, and which prayer should I offer for that?

Answer: A permanent solution should be sought not at the time of the incident but well before it occurs. For this, first, understand what is beyond everything. For instance, if the senses tempt you, there is something beyond them. If your mind allures you or your intellect becomes corrupt, there is something beyond them. What is it that transcends everything? It is the sense of beingness, the experience of the Self, your true nature, often referred to as the eternal presence. Everything else is its manifestation.

When you consistently ask yourself, "Who am I?" in every situation, and remain in the sense of beingness, you can witness every incident with detachment. This realization is the final tool, the permanent solution.

For this, you must have the understanding, awareness, and unwavering conviction of your true being. When you believe, "I am this body," your thoughts are confined to the realm of *Maya*. However, when you are aware that "I am not this body," the structure of your thoughts changes, giving rise to thoughts grounded in Truth rather than Maya.

When you use the final tool and ask yourself, "What is the highest choice I can make in this situation? Who am I that will make this choice?" then, even without making a choice, by adopting an attitude of "Watch, Wait with Wonder," you align with the highest choice. Therefore, first, awaken your awareness; then, whatever unfolds will be the best. Although it may not seem that way immediately, it will ultimately prove to be the best.

Let us understand this with an example. When one experiences anger, one thinks, "Anger has set in; what should I do now?" The answer is the same. Instead of contemplating when you are already angry, prepare well in advance that anger arises in the body; it is not occurring with who you truly are. This awakening serves as the antidote for anger; it is the final tool. If you maintain awareness of your true identity when anger sets in, you will neither suppress nor vent it on someone. Instead, you will observe it with detachment. By doing so, you will remain detached from anger and experience inner peace.

When you use this final tool in any situation, you become aware. You transcend your senses, mind, and intellect and attain the supreme state where your intellect gains discernment, and you bask in the delight of that discernment. Your mind dwells in the truth, and your senses become self-controlled. Otherwise, no matter how much you satiate your senses, you are left with a lingering sense of dissatisfaction.

For instance, suppose you spend the entire day watching a cricket match. At the end of the day, you honestly question yourself, "If I had not watched the match, how would it have mattered in my life? What have I truly gained by watching it?" This honest introspection will reveal the futility of spending your time in such avenues.

Many people don't ask the right questions to themselves, hence live a life of slumber. By asking the right questions to yourself, you can lead an awakened life.

Essence: Merely perceiving incidents with the right understanding as a detached witnesser is the highest choice in itself. The moment you clearly see, "I am not this body," you break free from the illusory thoughts that come with attachment to the body and revel in the experience of the Self.

21
The Essence of Challenges

 *The secret to becoming proficient in any field lies in consistent practice. Skilled players or artists master their respective fields not only because of their knowledge but also due to their regular practice to hone their expertise.*

Question: Where should my focus be in various situations?

Answer: The mind thinks, "I can stay focused only in some situations, not all of them." Now, replace this thought with a new thought, **"The various situations are challenges for me."**

For instance, consider a scenario where a singer is challenged: While singing, you may be exposed to the chatter of raindrops pelting on the roof, or people around you may engage in conversations, but you must continue to sing in tune.

Such challenges are deliberately designed for the singer to practice and stay focused amid various circumstances. Even the most proficient singers continue their practice in every situation, perceiving every situation as a challenge.

If you find yourself perplexed in a particular situation, treat it as a challenge, "How can I stay focused and stable even amid this situation? What strategies can I devise to stay aware even in such a situation?"

Even in the most challenging circumstances, when a player resolves, "I must set this world record," they commit themselves to practice diligently to attain their goal instead of lamenting their situation.

Hence, to maintain a consistent practice in all situations, inculcate some good habits. Contemplate after every situation, "What could I have done differently to improve it? Did I enjoy it or suffer?" If the answer is "I suffered," reflect on how you could have enjoyed it.

Until you confront a situation or challenge and assess it, you won't know how smoothly you can navigate through it. Therefore, refrain from holding any preconceived negative notions in your mind beforehand. If you wish to have any notions, let them be positive, such as, "I remain aware in every situation, which helps me stay focused," or "Divine power guides me every moment, so everything turns out to be the best." Adopting such positive notions will help cast aside any negative conditioning within you and embrace a new perspective where everything is easy and possible with practice.

Until such new affirmations are deeply ingrained in your subconscious mind, it may seem impossible to be constantly aware in every situation. Hence, consistently keep repeating this thought, **"This is indeed possible and easy."** Through consistent repetition, this thought will permeate your subconscious mind, manifesting it into reality.

> **Essence:** Through practice and with an elevated awareness, you can tide through every situation successfully. Embrace every situation as a challenge and tackle it with awareness. Have faith in your ability to confront and overcome these challenges and apply this practice to all future situations.

22
The Essence of Livelihood and Spirituality

 One who embraces the wisdom of the truth, the practice of meditation, and impersonal service, overcomes all shortcomings, whether one is a king or a common man.

Question: I often contemplate dedicating my entire life to serving the Truth (God), but I also think about my livelihood. Are these thoughts appropriate, and how can I strike a balance between the two?

Answer: Both thoughts are appropriate because you have assumed the form of this physical body here on earth. So, the first service is to take care of this body. Then, train your body in such a way that it advances towards the ultimate goal, which is to serve the truth (God), not the ego.

You need to earn your livelihood to sustain yourself in the world and engage in impersonal service alongside it. This will also help you in your livelihood goals.

Consider that you must complete a task in your office that requires two hours. However, when you embrace spiritual wisdom, the practice of meditation, and impersonal service in your life, it raises your level of consciousness. This helps you make decisions more thoughtfully, positively changes your behavior with people, and increases your alertness and efficiency. As a result, you will find yourself completing the task in just an hour, leaving you with an extra hour to dedicate to impersonal service without any hindrance. This way, you can strike a harmonious balance between your livelihood and impersonal service. By doing so, you will attain a greater sense of self-satisfaction and joy.

The most important aspect of impersonal service is the principle of "Let the service serve the server," signifying that the body rendering the service should get trained and help in the journey of stabilizing in the true Self.

When you are involved in worldly activities, sometimes you are praised, and sometimes, criticized, which serves to train your mind and body comprehensively. When your body is well-trained, you can effectively apply the spiritual teachings in the right way. Otherwise, without proper training, instead of reducing your ego, your impersonal service might inadvertently inflate it. Hence, it is essential to hone your skills, gain expertise in your chosen field of activity, and then work on the mind. Until your mind becomes trained, consistently practice activities such as listening to the truth, contemplation, reading, writing, and meditation. Once your mind is trained, you can make the right decision and progress toward serving the truth.

> **Essence:** Truth is eternal and omnipresent; it can be embraced everywhere, in every field. When you attain this conviction, it can become your inherent nature.
>
> When you are able to serve without ego, it will positively boost your lifestyle, competence, and efficiency. This will enable you to complete all your tasks efficiently within the scheduled time.
>
> There is a popular proverb that means, "Attain the one, and you will accomplish everything." Similarly, "Attain the true Self, the One, and you will attain everything."

23
The Essence of Understanding Strict Laws

 The power of prayer can eradicate all defilements in the world. All that is needed is sincerity and persistence in prayers.

Question: Are the defilements and wrong tendencies of the human mind responsible for the crimes and atrocities happening in the world today? Can strict laws alone prevent them? How can we get rid of them completely?

Answer: Strict laws are enacted to refrain people from committing crimes out of fear of penalty. While fear can control it to some extent, fear alone cannot entirely eliminate criminal tendencies. To achieve complete control, the level of understanding and consciousness of people needs to be elevated. Rules, regulations, and laws are in place to inculcate discipline in the environment of a country, city, or village, facilitating the smooth collective functioning of all external systems in a society.

To completely eliminate criminal tendencies, it is crucial to address the internal state or mindset of the individual. Improving the mindset means that the thought of committing the crime should not even occur to the criminal. This requires improving the mental and ideological health of society, primarily through spirituality.

Often, as new laws are made, new ways are also devised to break or bypass them. Some people even take pleasure in violating the law, adhering to the notion that "Laws are meant to be broken." However, this low level of pleasure is shallow, and to achieve a higher level of contentment, it is imperative to cultivate a deeper understanding.

Hence, contemplate: What is the current state of the world and its needs? What is my contribution to making it better? What is the best I can do to help fulfill the needs of the world?

People often have a common tendency to oppress those whom they consider weaker. If you consider yourself weak or others perceive you weak, understand that you are indirectly subjected to bear oppression. Hence, it is imperative to increase the understanding at every level of society. No one should consider themselves weak or excessively powerful. It is only when everyone has faith in humanity that a balance will be established in the world.

Today, people are trying to solve problems at a level lower than the level at which crimes are committed. Instead, they should first raise the level of consciousness and then try to solve the problems. By raising the understanding of people, it will become easier to make laws and follow them. With improved understanding, people would want to follow laws themselves. Hence, it is of utmost significance to elevate the understanding and level of consciousness of the legislators and the constituents for whom the laws are made. Only then will it become possible to eliminate criminal behavior and atrocities.

> **Essence:** Eliminate not the crime but the criminal mentality; eliminate not the sin but the tendency to sin and lead the society toward spirituality so that a state of peace is established.

24

The Essence of Creation Beyond Thoughts

 *Negativity leads you towards scarcity, while positivity leads you towards happiness and prosperity. Therefore, work upon your shortcomings instead of letting them become the cause of your sorrow*

Question: I feel disappointed when I face challenges at work due to either my own or others' irresponsibility, leading to a detrimental outcome. What should be my perspective in such negative situations?

Answer: Whenever any work comes to a halt, look at it from two perspectives.

1. Analyze what caused the work to stop, what were the obstacles, and how they have stopped the work.

2. Try to see what is being created in the unseen. If you reflect on the reasons why the work has been stalled, all the unseen possibilities will come to light. For example, if you are unable to progress in some field of activity, assess the kind of training you need to impart to your body, mind, and intellect. Considering it as an opportunity, take advantage of it.

In the realm of the unseen, some things come naturally and effortlessly, while others face obstacles. Things that are destined to manifest arrive effortlessly without any hindrance. However, when nature introduces obstacles, it signals that those things are not meant to be created yet.

Actually, obstacles arise due to conflict in inputs. When one is unclear about what one wants, one desires something internally while expressing something else externally, leading to a conflict in one's mind. Most often, people themselves are unaware of this internal conflict. In such instances, nature creates obstacles, difficulties, and hurdles in their path, causing their work to stall.

These events make them contemplate what they truly want. They need to first become one-sided, i.e., clearly decide whether they want to perform a particular task or not, whether they want a certain thing or not.

Everything in the world, whether in the process of creation or that has already manifested, is the result of a single-pointed prayer. A prayer is single-pointed when its intention, thought, feeling, and action are all perfectly aligned in one direction. Where there is misalignment between them, conflicts arise, and those tasks either do not manifest, or there is a delay in their manifestation.

We witness several positive and negative events in our surroundings. For instance, some people succeed in preventing terrorists from spreading terrorism, while some terrorists succeed in carrying out destructive acts. These accomplishments, good or bad, result from the certainty in their intentions and thoughts.

Those who succeed in preventing terrorism are clear and firm in their stance. However, those struggling with fear, doubt, or indecisiveness do not succeed in their actions. Thus, clarity of thought is crucial for achieving success and accomplishing tasks easily.

Manifestation in the unseen realm occurs only when one's thoughts are single-pointed and one-sided. When the mind is preoccupied with other things, the process of manifestation may experience delays or obstacles. Finally, the manifestation process is determined by the individual's thoughts and mindset.

While you may attribute delays in manifestations to external circumstances, people, or things, the root cause lies within you. Creations are shaped by internal laws. Hence, you are repeatedly asked to work on yourself first, and external aspects will automatically fall into place.

Things manifest based on the thoughts you entertain. Even if numerous people work timely and diligently on an external task, the work remains unfinished if there is resistance within you. Only when you have worked within yourself to resolve your inner conflict, the external work can be accomplished. Therefore, first, bring clarity to your thoughts.

Some people say, "We want to create something big," but if they lack the capability to handle it, the creation does not happen. Only when they develop the necessary capabilities, the tasks are accomplished easily. Hence, instead of blaming external factors, first work on the shortcomings in the situation.

Essence: To accomplish any task, you must possess the necessary capability and competence. To achieve that, introspect and contemplate the obstacles that arise in the work. If there are any conflicts in the mind, resolve them and bring clarity to your thoughts.

25
The Essence of Joy and Sorrow

 When the mind is functioning with thoughts of daily chores, it is called the intuitive mind. On the contrary, when the same mind is preoccupied with thoughts of judging, comparing, and evaluating, it is known as the contrast mind.

Question: Why do we face sorrow, problems, and adversity in our life? Is there a permanent solution to them?

Answer: The term "contrast" signifies opposites, such as black and white. You may feel happy at one moment, and then experience sorrow the next moment. This represents a contrast. Sorrow serves as a reminder that you were happy. Otherwise, amid happiness, you fail to recognize its significance. It is only when sorrow sets in and happiness departs that you truly comprehend the happiness you had. It is like realizing the presence of light only after it is switched off.

Although we have been gifted a human life, we often fail to cherish it. Have you ever wondered how happy you should be being born a human? No, you haven't because you often fail to realize the importance of what has been bestowed upon you. Hence, the role of contrast becomes pivotal in life.

When you are ill, you realize the importance of good health. When someone askes for both your eyes in return for one million dollars, you would refuse. Even if they make the offer for one eye, you would still decline. Why? Because you know your eyes are priceless.

A poor man was unhappy with his financial condition. One day, holding an empty bag, he went to the market, thinking, "I have nothing, while others have so much." Just then, a thief snatched his bag and ran away. He chased the thief and got his bag back. Upon getting hold of the bag, he felt immense joy and became more alert. Now, he started taking care of the bag while walking.

A little while ago, he was unhappy, claiming he had nothing. Even though he had an empty bag, it was only when it was snatched away that he realized he had something that was taken away. Similarly, we may have many things, but instead of focusing on what we have, we often focus on what we do not have and bring sorrow.

There is an intuitive mind and a contrast mind within each of us. Every task is effortlessly accomplished with the intuitive mind. However, the contrast mind casts doubts on everything and divides everything into two by indulging in judgment and comparison. Animals only have an intuitive mind, so they lead a peaceful life. The contrast mind creates a disturbance in human life, and the value of peace is also realized because of this contrast mind. By demonstrating the unrest created by the contrast mind, we are guided back to reality.

Until the contrast comes into play, people do not contemplate; hence, it has its own significance. Eventually, a time will come when you will declare, "I don't need the contrast anymore. I have learned my lessons." But until then, the role of contrast continues.

Essence: After learning the lessons of life, we stabilize in the state of permanent bliss. After that, the role of the contrast mind and the sorrow it creates ends.

26
The Essence of Confusion and Clarity

 Whenever you make a choice, take a moment to reflect: "Which choice is apt at this moment, and what is the choice I am making? Is it a lower, higher, or the highest choice?" By adopting this approach, you will succeed at decision-making.

Question: Thoughts play a vital role in our life. But which thoughts should we prioritize to attain clarity instead of confusion? How can we differentiate between the thoughts arising from the mind and those emerging from the intellect?

Answer: It is not enough to recognize the thoughts arising from the mind or the intellect. It is also essential to recognize the thoughts arising from the power of discernment and the true Self. *Viveka,* or discerning power, helps us discriminate between the truth and the untruth.

One can choose to ascend from the lower to the highest level of consciousness or descend from the highest to the lower levels of consciousness. Wisdom lies in making choices that are always aligned with the highest.

The extent to which you have honestly reflected on the following aspects determine whether your problems get resolved or become more complicated:

- The state of consciousness in your body-mind.
- The perspective and understanding with which you perceive a problem.
- Your ability to consider all the available options when making a decision.
- The specific choice you make.
- Your awareness about the potential consequences of that choice.

Otherwise, it would be like standing in darkness while assessing the mind and intellect. Relying solely on the mind and intellect in such darkness might lead one to believe they have made a clever decision. However, the mind and intellect require the illuminating light of the consciousness to perceive the highest choice. After perceiving the highest choice, the mind and intellect require Viveka to embrace it, and Viveka awakens with understanding. In other words, the highest choice can be made when the mind and intellect are accompanied by consciousness and Viveka.

It is comparable to the sufficiency of light in a room, which decides how well someone with good eyesight can perceive their surroundings. What they understand depends on the quantum of light and the quality of their perception; and what they understand, in turn, determines their approach and actions.

In short, the state of Viveka within one's body-mind governs how their mind and intellect are put to use. When the level of consciousness is low and Viveka remains dormant, decisions are made from a state of ignorance, often leading to confusion and complications. However, when the level of consciousness is high and Viveka is sharp and vigilant, decisions are made with awareness, leading to clarity and ease with which issues get resolved. Both possibilities are available to us.

Essence: Decisions driven by the mind and intellect may sometimes lead to dilemmas and solutions at times, whereas decisions taken in the light of awareness and guided by Viveka only bring the joy of resolution.

27
The Essence of Helplessness

 *Whenever you get the thought, "Bad things always happen to me," take a pause and affirm, "Whatever happens to me ultimately turns out to be good!" Consider this as a divine ordainment, a declaration from God.*

Question: What is helplessness?

Answer: Most people often feel helpless when faced with a difficult situation. It is a state of dilemma that is very much like either jumping into a crocodile-infested lake or confronting a relentless charging lion.

In this state of helplessness arising from ignorance and a lack of faith, they find it difficult to maintain patience. At times, the feeling of despair can become so overwhelming that some do not hesitate even to embrace death. In fact, helplessness is the extreme lack of faith, borne from ignorance and misunderstanding.

Contemplate whether one really reaches a point of utter helplessness. If one can use this helplessness as a catalyst for practicing deep introspection and Sadhana, it can serve as a powerful reminder of the divine presence within them.

When you find yourself unable to navigate a situation, unsure of what to do, how to do it, or what is right or wrong, take a moment to sit quietly with closed eyes and stop your incessant thinking. This is essential, especially when you are in a state of helplessness and struggle to comprehend anything. When you stabilize yourself in this manner, you unknowingly surrender; from that state of surrender, a faint glimmer of light begins to emerge. This ray of light will appear only when you stop your restless movements and stay calm and peaceful. Then, this little ray of light will guide you, illuminating your path ahead.

If you can think properly, redirect your thinking, and reflect: What is the worst outcome that can unfold in this state of helplessness? What is the worst-case scenario that can happen during this visit to Earth? If you believe that you can harness even the worst-case scenario as a catalyst to create a beautiful opportunity, then the grip of helplessness will no longer trouble you.

Once you grasp this understanding, you can transform helplessness into a sacred gift. While feeling helpless is not a pleasant experience, it does serve as a form of divine guidance. This is the moment that demands complete surrender. By giving this uncomfortable feeling, God is awakening you, "Change the course of your thoughts so that I can give you a good feeling. You carry out your part; I shall do mine, and we will resolve the problem together. Have a little faith. This state of helplessness is temporary, not permanent. So, don't get entangled in it; keep progressing."

When you regard the feeling of helplessness as something wrong, it only intensifies your distress. Therefore, in moments of helplessness, affirm to yourself, "It is a fantastic situation. No matter what I do, there could be losses, but it is still a remarkable state that I can learn from."

In moments of distress, you might exclaim, "It is easier said than done, as only the wounded can truly understand the pains of the wound. I alone know what I have been through." Regardless of what you say, this is the remedy, though it may seem bitter. There may be times when you can do very little. Just place your faith in God, follow the guidance received, and soon the feeling of helplessness will subside.

Essence: In this ever-changing world, nothing is permanent. When faced with challenges, confront them with the understanding that "Just as it has come, so shall it pass." By adopting this perspective, half your pain will vanish. Then, observe how the problem naturally gets resolved on its own. During moments of excessive restlessness, find solace in prayers.

Furthermore, problems and difficulties come in life to shake you up so that you are compelled to change your existing patterns, mend your ways, and evolve. In this process, your level of awareness rises, enabling you to uncover the hidden mysteries underlying these events.

28

The Essence of Completeness in the Family

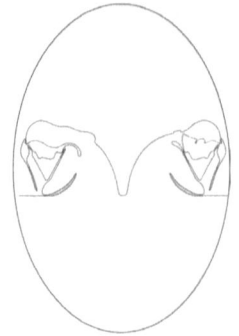

 *To foster harmony in the family, it is essential to establish a platform where there is no bitterness in relationships and where sweetness prevails. This platform in the family will facilitate better understanding and eliminate conflicts.*

Question: There is a lot of conflicts and discord with my spouse. How can we reduce this?

Answer: To reduce mutual differences, start by accepting each other exactly as you are. Understand that each one has a distinct mindset and nature, making them unique. No one is exactly like the other, yet they complement one another. Secondly, nurture open communication in the family to reduce discord and achieve completion within the family.

For achieving completion, two key aspects are involved.

1. Openly express any concerns or thoughts that trouble you regarding the other person, using kind words to them.
2. Openly acknowledge and appreciate their positive qualities. We seldom do this. Take time to share the aspects that you admire about each other.

For example, if the wife is an excellent cook and the husband relishes her meals, he can delightfully compliment her by saying, "I enjoy the delicious food you prepare" or "You make this particular dish so well." In this way, husband and wife can achieve completion in their relationship, deepen their mutual understanding, and become supportive well-wishers for each other.

Often, we refrain from achieving completion due to our own fears. We feel that openly sharing our feelings with the other person may hurt them or praising them may make us vulnerable to domination. Consequently, instead of conveying our genuine feelings, we often say something different, which only aggravates the conflicts rather than resolving them. To achieve completion, it is crucial to express our genuine feelings openly.

Women often harbor a hidden desire for the other person to intuitively grasp their needs without them explicitly and clearly stating it. However, they should set aside this expectation and lovingly communicate what they want.

There are certain principles to be followed when pursuing completion. When both partners work toward achieving this, the foremost rule is to avoid reacting immediately to the other person. Allow a period of 12 hours to reflect on what has been heard and then respond in a composed and patient manner. This approach makes for a calm and considerate way to address the situation.

While pursuing completion, understand that you are not blaming the other person but conveying your emotions. For example, a husband striving for completion with his wife might say, "I want to achieve completeness with you. The other day, you said something that I did not like. I may not have fully understood your perspective, but it hurt me. Thank you for allowing me an opportunity to share my feelings."

As soon as you openly and honestly share your suppressed emotions, you become open, and the other person also becomes receptive to acknowledge their own mistakes.

Take care of some other aspects as well while pursuing completion. For example, if it appears that the situation is worsening during the pursuit of completion, take prompt action to stop it. Ensure you express your thoughts using positive words to prevent the other person from interpreting it as a complaint.

At times, some people may unintentionally slip into a complaining mode. For instance, they may grumble, "Why did you misbehave with me on that occasion? I found it unpleasant. It would have been better if you had acted differently."

Such a complaining tone can worsen the situation. When seeking completion, you must use kind words in a gentle manner. Your intention should be to resolve the conflict, promote understanding, and eliminate complaints. Doing so creates space for the other person to achieve completion and openly express their thoughts.

If the other person is not actively pursuing completion, accept their choice. Don't compel them to do it. Initiate the pursuit of completion yourself because **only those who actively seek it, can help others achieve it.**

At the end of the pursuit of completion, remember to convey the bottom line to the other person, which marks the success of this pursuit. Tell them, "Despite these trivial day-to-day issues, I like you, I love you." This fundamental aspect can also be shared at the beginning of your conversation.

If both partners follow these guiding principles to communicate with one another, they will indeed find themselves saying, "No conflicts, only gratitude!" Upon achieving completion, they will feel grateful toward each other.

> **Essence:** Whether within your family or among friends, strive for completion with each other to resolve conflicts. Try to understand each other, as this enhanced understanding will allow your mutual love to flourish.

29

The Essence of Information Received in Life

 If you want to bring about a positive transformation in your life, keep the company of people whose motto is "Self-improvement and upliftment of others."

Question: Engaging in negative discussions about someone in their absence is a form of third-person talk. I often hesitate to discourage people who engage in such third-person talk for fear of straining my relationship with them. There is also a concern about missing some relevant information if I do not hear what they have to say. What should I do in such situations?

Answer: This is a case of contradictory prayers. On one hand, you do not want to spoil your relationship; and on the other, you want to be informed of everything happening around you. You do not wish to miss out on anything – you wish to avoid discomfort and also avail of the benefits.

First and foremost, develop the faith that the information you need will come to you from the universe, no matter what the medium is. If you believe that only certain people can provide you with information, it is a limitation of your thinking that you must overcome. Furthermore, eliminate the misconception that you extracted the information by manipulating your communication. Actually, that information was meant to be received by you; hence it reached you.

Once you gain clarity in your approach, things begin to get resolved. You can politely tell the other person, "Such third-person conversations trouble me. Hence, please do not engage with me in such conversations about people in their absence." Avoid belittling the other person by tutoring them on how they are doing the wrong thing, or proving how you are being superior by avoiding third-party conversations. Instead, if you communicate your preferences clearly and directly, people will gradually understand that you do not appreciate such discussions, and they will slowly reduce them while conversing with you.

If you have clarity about the company you want to keep, you empower that choice. Every event that comes your way has the potential to empower you, but sometimes, you lose sight of what you have to empower in that moment. You may only remember, "I don't want this," causing your focus to remain on what is undesirable. As a result, nature repeatedly brings such undesirable experiences into your life.

Hence, affirm to yourself what you want to empower in your life, for example, "In my life, I want people who appreciate others, speak positively about their virtues, and discuss growth." By doing so, you will naturally attract only such people into your life. Consider it as nature's blessing bestowed upon you and enjoy it.

Otherwise, conflicting prayers can lead to confusion. You want something, yet at the same time, you don't want it. You harbor discomfort with such matters, yet simultaneously, you find something appealing about them. This internal contradiction can leave you feeling uncertain and confused. To gain clarity, ask yourself, "Have

I reached a state where the absence of such information would not significantly impact my life?"

For instance, daily newspapers contain so much information, and yet you remain contented even without reading it. Similarly, even if you do not receive the anticipated information about the third person, it would not affect you, and you could still remain happy.

If you hold beliefs that "Without certain information, I won't get promoted, make progress, or achieve success," you will get stuck in them. Therefore, you must first step out of these limiting beliefs and foster the faith that "Whatever is genuinely essential for you will naturally come your way."

Be very clear about what you genuinely want. If you seek love, joy, and peace, you must decide the attitude with which you should be present in various situations. If you honestly reflect, you will receive guidance from within.

> **Essence:** Gain a clear understanding of what you really want and continue to empower those desires by reaffirming your intentions repeatedly.

30
The Essence of Parenting

 Children are the offspring of God rather than possessions of human beings. God has entrusted parents with the role of their caretakers, not owners. Therefore, parents should nurture pure love for their children, devoid of attachment.

Question: My daughter is of marriageable age. I keep worrying about when she will get married and how will her life partner be. Please guide me in this matter.

Answer: Firstly, dwell in a state of higher consciousness and perform positive prayers. Believe in yourself, have faith in the divine plan, and remain connected to the inner joy of your beingness in every situation.

Generally, there are no defined age limits for marriage; it varies for everyone. Everyone searches for their life partner or goal according to their divine plan. Some may marry at an early age, some later in life, while others may choose not to marry at all.

Hence, we are often unaware of the reasons and the underlying divine plan behind whatever happens in the world. Terms like "early marriage" and "late marriage" are used for convenience, but in reality, there are no such fixed rules.

In some Indian communities, girls may get married at a young age, perhaps as early as eighteen. In some villages, they may be married even earlier. In contrast, urban children prioritize their careers and higher education over marriage. They choose to get married after they become financially independent. Thus, the timing of marriage is significantly influenced by place, culture, priorities, and environmental factors.

In certain households, youth are free to decide when they want to marry, while in others, their elders are responsible for deciding on their behalf.

Therefore, understand that all beings are part of the divine. We don't know the complete purpose of our lives. Hence, consider your children as the embodiment of Lord Krishna and yourself as Mother Yashoda. Render selfless love to your children as Yashoda did for Lord Krishna. Regardless of whether and when your children choose to marry, ensure you love them unconditionally from the bottom of your heart and care for them to the best of your ability.

Children have a life of their own and their life purpose to fulfill. Their prayers reflect their unique paths, and their life is shaped accordingly. Have faith that everything will fall into place once they are internally prepared for the next scene of their life. Pray for their bright future and watch it happen with patience and a sense of wonder.

Essence: Love children selflessly and safeguard yourself from unnecessary worries. With this, they will progress according to their divine plan.

31
The Essence of Gain and Loss

 One who leads an impersonal and selfless life does not fear losing anything.

Question: I could not visit my in-laws for many years due to certain conflicts and disagreements. However, I always prayed for the right moment to come. Now, circumstances have changed, and I have decided to revisit them. However, I am anxious about whether the situation will repeat. Please guide me on this.

Answer: Have faith and do not let the doubt, "Will I ever be able to live in harmony at my in-laws' house?" overpower your faith. If this thought arises, let it go immediately. Always focus on "What should happen" instead of worrying about "What will happen." Prejudice and fear only create obstacles in life. Hence, set aside such thoughts and realign yourself with the divine flow.

Some fears serve as precautions. For instance, when you are about to perform on stage, it is natural to feel anxious and afraid, as these emotions steer you to be well-prepared. However, do not entertain baseless fears or harbor any negative feelings. Avoid anticipating that something will inevitably go wrong, and refrain from prematurely labeling any situation. Move ahead with the same faith that has brought forth the present situation.

Now, you have noticed the improved situation at your in-laws' place and decided to visit them. Maintain this faith in your intuition. When you were born, you didn't have any teeth, but now you have thirty-two. Even if you lose a tooth, you will still have thirty-one left. You have not lost anything here but have only gained thirty-one! If you look at every situation with such a positive outlook, you will realize that you have **everything to gain and nothing to lose**.

Even if something negative happens, you still have nothing to lose because you possess the resilience, enabling you to always create anew. Therefore, there is no need to worry. Keep praying and enhancing your abilities consistently.

When you become capable, no matter how many setbacks you receive, you will bounce back and even help others. Hence, don't be afraid. Your capabilities honed through life experiences will help you to keep a positive outlook on life.

> **Essence:** After deciding to do something, set aside all doubts and fears. Have faith in your conviction because you have nothing to lose and everything to gain.

32

The Essence of Making the Right Decision

 Before making any decision, take time to conquer your fears or get rid of them by making small decisions.

Question: I'm a divorcee and wish to remarry, but I prefer to marry an unmarried girl. However, my family feels that I should not set such a condition. What should I do? I'm confused.

Answer: Before stepping into a new scene, it is essential to detach from your past completely. Begin by honestly reflecting, "What aspects of myself, what thoughts, what seeds did I sow, what were my actions that led to the previous scene in my life?"

Give yourself ample time to contemplate all these matters so that the clarity you gain can liberate you entirely from the influence of the past.

Always remember that before praying for a new beginning, seek a new understanding from the lessons learned from past experiences. Then, pray for the best possible outcome and patiently wait until you receive the answer to your prayers. Additionally, pay close attention to your behavior and thoughts. Decode and grasp any subtle indications you encounter during your prayer, and then make your decisions accordingly. Have faith that your prayers will craft the course of events for you.

Refrain from applying any extra force by insisting that "This should happen, this shouldn't happen," and avoid entertaining any negative thoughts. Keep your focus solely on alignment with the divine flow of life in your prayers, and never let go of the "Happy Hat," the feeling of happiness.

If any fear, doubt, or greed arises, let go of it. For this, give yourself some time to introspect and examine your emotions. When certain internal aspects fall into place within you, external matters will also work out with ease. The decisions made with a pure and peaceful mind will prove right and turn useful in the long term.

During prayer, detach yourself from the outcome; if such an attachment exists, let go of it. Then, whatever is meant for you will naturally unfold.

> **Essence:** When venturing into previously failed endeavors, do not let the fear of failure cast a shadow. Instead, gather lessons from the past and continue to pray in the present for the envisaged future.

33
The Essence of True Help

 In relationships, it is essential to care for each other, nurture each other's growth, and foster independence. This way, you and your loved ones can live happily.

Question: I have a friend who is speech and hearing impaired. He married twice but has not been able to become a father. He has received a proposal from a divorced woman with a daughter. However, none of his relatives support this alliance. The girl's family wants me to intervene, take responsibility, and facilitate the marriage. I am unable to decide whether I should help him or not.

Answer: Some people venture to resolve others' issues and, rather than resolving them, end up getting entangled in those issues themselves. Therefore, it is essential to bring clarity within yourself before solving any problem. If you find yourself confused to decide on the next course of action, keep it on hold for now.

You receive indications from within about the tasks that you can smoothly accomplish, and you feel a sense of ease with the thought of undertaking them or performing them. If you do not experience this sense of ease or lack clear indications from within, don't proceed with those tasks right away.

Whenever you help someone, whether a friend or a family member, decide the extent to which you will help. One form of help is when you see a hungry person, you catch some fish and feed them. While your intention is good, it does not offer a permanent solution to their hunger. What will you do if you find them hungry again the next day? It is wiser to teach them how to fish on their own. This is the right kind of help as it provides a lasting solution to satiate their hunger.

Another form of help is to offer advice. For instance, if you have a higher understanding, you may offer advice to someone to resolve their problem. Once you have given advice, your role should end. You may explain the pros and cons of the advice to them, but you should leave the decision-making to them. Thus, you avoid getting caught up in the process of problem-solving. It is often observed that when people see your readiness to help, they may begin to expect more.

Therefore, if someone is relying on you to make their decision, do not encourage such dependency. This is appropriate for both you and the other person.

> **Essence:** When you find yourself in a state of confusion, it is best to avoid making decisions for others. You can help others to a certain extent but do not make them dependent on you.

34

The Essence of Discord in the Family

Ninety percent of issues in human relationships can be resolved when people begin to talk with one another instead of talking about one another. This not only resolves their problems but also nurtures an environment of love, joy, and peace.

Question: My mother-in-law is orthodox by nature. She follows traditional beliefs and customs. She wants me to keep my head and face veiled—a custom prevalent in India. If I oppose, my husband is upset. What should I do in this situation?

Answer: Conflicts arise in most households due to the belief, "He should not do this; She should not say that; I should be free to do what I want; No one should interfere in my matters," and so on.

In this case, you feel that you should be allowed to stay without the veil, but you cannot. This inner conflict between your behavior and thoughts causes distress because you are unable to accept the situation wholeheartedly.

Every family has their traditions and principles. Their food, clothing, customs, and way of living are different. Therefore, first accept the way things are. Instead of harboring complaints, cultivate a forgiving attitude and keep praying for what you want in your life.

Many believe that if they accept any wrong custom or something they dislike, the situation will worsen, and they will remain unhappy throughout their lives. However, this is not true. Accepting the situation boosts your inner strength. In this case, you must accept it as the family's tradition and then pray to stay unveiled.

Moreover, lovingly share your feelings with someone who understands you. They could be your husband, sister-in-law, or some other confidante. This can help facilitate bringing a change at home. After that, you can share your concerns with your mother-in-law. If she still insists, try not to harbor any ill feelings toward her but have firm faith that "It's just a matter of a few days; my mother-in-law will agree to it eventually." If you respect your mother-in-law, she will also respect your perspective one day. When she observes that many other families in her surroundings are no longer following the custom of staying veiled, she may reconsider her stance.

If you hold on to negative feelings, the situation can worsen. If you keep pondering, "I'm always confined to the veil because of these people. My life has become hell. I cannot live freely," nature acknowledges and blesses these thoughts, "So be it," and the situation persists. Hence, accept it with this perspective, "Today, this is the situation, but it need not remain the same tomorrow. The beautiful life I aspire to live will manifest." Also, hold on to your happy state. Very soon, you will witness a miraculous change in your life.

Accept the present and have faith in your prayers. Then transformation will happen soon. Even if you learn this much, whatever may be your present circumstances, they will change in the days to come.

> **Essence:** Wholeheartedly accept the situation as it is without complaints or unhappiness. In due course, you will surely get to experience the desired outcome.

35
The Essence of the Demise of Loved Ones

 Fear of death arises from ignorance about death. On attaining the knowledge of death, death teaches us the art of living.

Question: How do we overcome the mental trauma caused by the demise of a loved one?

Answer: Such unexpected incidents shake most people. The sudden loss disrupts the setup of their homes and causes them profound grief. People get overwhelmed by negative thoughts and find it difficult to move ahead in life. However, if they change their perspective of looking at such situations, they will not be affected by the negative thoughts.

As regards death, the entire society perceives it as a mourning incident. The way death is perceived needs to be changed completely. Various rituals and practices related to death are intended to help the families cope with the grief. However, when they are deeply attached to the deceased, they find it difficult to let go of the sorrow.

Constantly grieving for the departed one may prevent them from fully embracing their relationships and opportunities in the present life. If they move beyond this, they can be instrumental in helping others overcome their grief. Otherwise, their beliefs can keep them unhappy throughout their life. In such a situation, they need to look around, communicate with people who have gone through such incidents before, inquire about their experiences, how they overcame their sorrow, and learned from their experiences. Whatever has happened cannot be changed; it can only be accepted. Acceptance helps reduce the sorrow.

In fact, death is a method of nature by which the *Leela* of this world continues. With this method, one raises their vibrations to express themselves in the subtle world. The death of the gross body serves as a means to transition to the subtle body. However, it becomes a reason for sorrow because they can no longer see or interact with the departed one. Instead of succumbing to sadness after witnessing death, one should recognize this as the means to proceed on the extended journey of their earthly life.

Emotions are independent of time and space. They easily get conveyed from life on Earth to life after death. When one becomes clear about this, they can come to terms with their sorrowful emotions, choose to entertain positive feelings for the departed one, and pray for their smooth onward journey. Additionally, they can live their earthly life with love, joy, and peace.

> **Essence:** You can live a peaceful life by contemplating and understanding death. Just as you have accepted life, come to terms with death, and realize who you truly are, beyond the gross body that perishes and the subtle body that continues its journey. This will help you overcome your grief.

36
The Essence of the Impact of Words

 Positive words have vibrations that can bestow good health. Hence, always use optimistic and inspiring words. Keep humming the words like love, joy, and contentment.

Question: According to the science of the mind, using the word "no" does not create any specific mental image. Hence the word "no" does not impress upon the subconscious mind. However, when we repeatedly tell children, "You cannot do this," how does their mind get programmed with "I cannot do it?"

Answer: People always feel confused about this matter. It is important to understand that one of them is a prayer, while the other is a limiting belief. Although both sentences appear similar, prayer and belief follow different rules and are recorded with nature differently.

When the word "no" is used in prayer, it does not leave a lasting impression on the subconscious mind. However, the vibrations of the word "no" have a telling effect when used as a part of beliefs or presumptions. These are two different things.

For instance, when you say, "I am not the body," you state the reality and describe the truth by using the word "not." However, once you have attained the knowledge of the truth, you would not say, "I should not become the body," instead, you would say, "I should live as the true Self." There is a difference between both statements. Let us understand this further with a few more examples.

"I don't want a small car" is a wrong prayer. The right prayer would be, "I want a big car." The underlying belief is, "I can't afford a big car." The right self-talk would be, "If I do well, I can surely afford a big car."

Similarly, when parents tell their child, "You cannot lift so much weight," it becomes their limiting belief, and they internalize it as the truth. However, if the truth is explained to the child, "Right now, since you are small, you cannot lift this weight. But, when you grow up, you will be able to lift it easily." Then, no belief or preconceived notion is formed in the child's mind. The difference lies in the way the message is conveyed.

Whenever you use the word "no," it is essential to consider the context in which it is used. Depending on the context, its usage and consequences will vary. Therefore, before using the word "no," first reflect on its implications.

Let's understand how the word "no" affects our prayers with the help of an example. A student wants to pass an exam. But due to a lack of knowledge of the science of mind, they unknowingly pray, "I don't want to fail the exam." In this case, since the word "no" is not imprinted in the subconscious mind, the word "fail" gets highlighted and imprinted. Consequently, the probability of the student failing the exam increases. At such times, the right prayer would be, "I would like to see myself successful." As the focus is on success, it will be imprinted in the subconscious mind, guiding the student toward success.

This is a profound point; let us understand it with another example.

Consider a student who says, "I don't think I will pass the exam." Although the word "no" does not get imprinted, the focus is on the word "pass." Every word has its own vibration, and it keeps impacting the subconscious mind. In this case, the negative vibrations of the word "no" weaken the student's confidence, resulting in their failing the exam. Instead, if the student says, "Everyone who studies gets through the exam, I too will achieve success if I study." Then they will indeed become successful.

You need to be alert and aware to understand this point. Only then can you comprehend the hidden feelings, beliefs, and vibrations underlying each word.

> **Essence:** Before expressing, it is essential to know the consequences of your words. If your words are going to plant limiting beliefs or preconceived notions in the listener or reinforce their existing beliefs or notions, you need to be mindful and empower the right words in your prayers.

37
The Essence of Mental Stability

 When the mind is illumined with positive thoughts in every situation, it becomes filled with zest and enthusiasm, even in overtly challenging circumstances.

Question: My mind becomes restless in some situations. How can I ensure that it stays stable in every situation?

Answer: The level of consciousness varies for everyone. So, nature uses different ways to impart lessons to everyone. Consider a metaphorical ladder where people with lower consciousness at the bottom, those with medium consciousness in the middle, and those with the highest consciousness at the top.

Nature employs challenging methods to teach people with a lower level of consciousness because they cannot grasp subtle indications. For example, when someone suffers indigestion due to overeating, they resolve, "I won't commit this mistake again," only to get back to their old ways again. Then, nature teaches them by making them endure a critical illness, shaking them out of their indulgence.

Those with a medium level of consciousness do not have to be taught in such difficult ways. They understand what needs to be done next, even when they face minor problems. With resolve, they make arrangements that help them remember those lessons. They comprehend how nature operates and set up systems that not only benefit them but others, too.

Those with a higher level of consciousness do not necessarily undergo such hardships. They gain insights by observing others suffer. The Sikh Guru Arjun Dev Ji, while in prison before death, contemplated, "An army should be commissioned to prevent people from suffering extreme atrocities to ensure their lives become worthwhile." He envisioned that his sacrifice would benefit many others. So, he endured the atrocities inflicted by those with lower consciousness.

People with a higher level of consciousness possess the foresight to anticipate what lies ahead. They do not wait for problems to jolt them into action; instead, they proactively become aware and consistently sow the seeds for the future.

Nature alerts some people through some incidents while it prepares others to face some potential incidents in the future. Some remain unaffected despite going through incidents, while others become aware just by watching the news.

We must contemplate and pray for such elevated thinking to permeate our consciousness so that we can envision right away what we will be able to comprehend from higher consciousness.

Nature gives opportunity to everyone. As your wisdom increases, so does your receptivity. With wisdom and receptivity, you will be liberated from the restless mind, leading you to mental stability.

> **Essence:** While people with lower consciousness learn through hardships, those with higher consciousness become aware by observing others' distress. They practice self-control and help others. So, raise your level of consciousness with prayer and contemplation to develop your foresight and foster mental stability.

38

The Essence of Freedom from Discord in Relationships

 Relationships can be strengthened with unconditional love, sacrifice, forgiveness, and understanding.

Question: What is the higher perspective to view discord in relationships?

Answer: Some people may overlook the rifts in relationships as trivial matters. However, a wise one understands that these rifts affect not only the concerned ones but the entire world.

In fact, there is only one vibration in the entire universe, and we all are connected through that vibration.

When something happens in one corner of the world, its vibrations are felt across the globe. Yet, we often try to isolate ourselves from it by thinking, "It has not happened in our country." However, it impacts everyone, sooner or later.

For instance, when a tsunami approaches or a new epidemic emerges somewhere, the entire population has to bear the consequences. We have recently observed how the COVID-19 pandemic originated in one region, spread, and affected the entire world.

Every country has its distinct characteristics. Some countries may be hyperactive, some lethargic, while others equanimous. They have their own effect on the society at large. Similarly, people sharing the same zodiac sign have their own effects. Moreover, the people with whom we live and the decisions of those around us also influence us.

However, you need not be disappointed or distressed about this. Instead, you can develop awareness and awaken yourself with understanding. Such matters do not affect those who are aware and conscious. They lead a relaxed life with the conviction, **"I am dear to God; no fear can touch me!"**

It is imperative to be aware first. With awareness, you can keep yourself detached and free from these influences. Additionally, abstain yourself from activities that will disrupt the balance of the surrounding environment. Instead, seek forgiveness to eliminate discords in relationships and wholeheartedly forgive others.

> **Essence:** Although distinct, we are all connected. We experience things in a similar way, although our expressions may differ. Raise awareness to such an extent that the external events and other things happening around you do not distract you. Also, avoid becoming a cause of trouble for others.

39

The Essence of Liberation from Sorrow

 Whenever you encounter a problem, first become happy and then resolve the problem. This will help you discover the most apt and straightforward way to resolve the problem.

Question: Why do I experience so much sorrow? Can I ever attain a state of liberation from all sorrows?

Answer: Sorrow does not come to sadden us but to awaken us. Actually, sorrow is a kind of feedback, but when we label it as "sorrow", we get entangled in it.

Just as the term "problem" is not inherently troublesome. It is merely a container meant to deliver a solution sent by God. Unfortunately, at the mere sight of the container, one immediately labels it as a problem, ignoring the concealed solution that needs to be uncovered. The container is very robust, so the solution is safely kept till it is unraveled. However, people often become deluded by the container and perceive it as a problem, thus taking a long time to unpack it. As a result, they fail to recognize the solution hidden within the problem. This happens due to their skewed perspective that is shaded by limiting beliefs they have borrowed from the world. These beliefs intrude into their subconscious mind and cause them sorrow.

Therefore, instead of considering the problem as a problem, it helps to see it as a package containing the solution. Hence, don't feel intimidated by the external façade of the so-called problem. The problem comes to deliver the solution to you. Shift your focus away from the problem and receive the solution. With this perspective, the solution hidden in any problem begins to unravel by itself.

Similarly, instead of referring to sorrow as sorrow, consider it as feedback. God gives you the feeling of sorrow only to indicate how aligned or misaligned you are with Him. Perceiving the situation positively is a grace because it indicates that you are indeed aligned with God. When you fall out of this alignment, sorrow comes to remind you of that.

In order to regain your alignment, reflect on the grace bestowed on your life so far, what you have received so far to be grateful for, the futility of what you have lost, the utility of what you have gained, and all the blessings that have made you feel contented so far. As you contemplate these points, you will observe that you have regained your alignment with God, and the reasons for sorrow begin to dissolve. Thus, the sorrowful incidents occur in your life to teach you the art of solving problems by staying in divine alignment.

God is teaching you to remain happy at all times. He wants you to be in a state where you are always aligned. Hence, this entire *Leela*, the game of this illusory world, goes on. So, perceive and receive these incidents gracefully with the faith that everything is happening for your awakening.

With this understanding, observe your mind's chatter amid problems. Once you grasp this art, you will attain mastery in perceiving every incident the right way. Your mind will remain stable in every situation. Once you attain this state, you will experience the power of grand thinking.

With grand thinking, you think for the benefit of everyone, bringing well-being and happiness to everyone, including yourself. With narrow thinking, you think only for yourself. Hence, understand the power of grand thinking and maintain such a perspective.

When you maintain a positive perspective even in adverse situations, incidents empower you, and your life purpose is realized.

Essence: Sorrow is merely a feedback that tells you that you have fallen out of alignment with God. Learn to observe your mind's chatter and count your blessings to regain your alignment. The sorrowful situations will dissolve in due course.

40
The Essence of Detachment

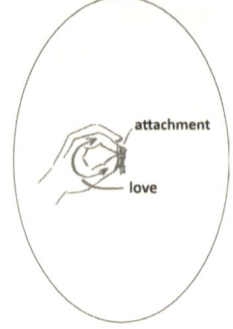

What you perceive as "mine" actually belongs to God. Consider that God has lent it to you for use as long as it remains with you. Enjoy it, express gratitude, yet refrain from forming undue attachment to it.

Question: Is it possible to let go of attachments?

Answer: Certainly, it becomes possible with self-introspection. The human mind tends to get attached to anything it comes in contact with, whether with animals like dogs, cats, or even non-living things. Attachment has become an integral part of human life.

The Buddha, through self-introspection, realized the fundamental truth that attachment is the root cause of human suffering. He witnessed attachment at the core of all thoughts, emotions, and desires that arose within him when he encountered various incidents. This awakened his self-awareness, and he realized that people need to attain this wisdom to be liberated from this hidden sorrow.

God created the human mind only to experience permanent, unconditional happiness. However, man gets entangled in illusory worldly pleasures, leading to the formation of attachments.

Imagine you are given a toy. When you turn it on, you forget your name, but as soon as you turn it off, you remember it. When you experience this, you feel ecstatic to have such a unique toy for your amusement. Yet, if engrossed in it, you forget to turn it off and cannot remember your name anymore. In such a case, the toy dominates you, and you become attached to it. Similarly, the mind, like the toy, was created for your happiness, but you have become so attached to it that you have forgotten your true Self.

Attachment was used in this creation to perpetuate the divine play. The entire arrangement has been designed so that as you realize who you truly are, the remembrance persists, and attachment naturally diminishes on its own. Then, you won't need to fight attachment; instead, you will begin to comprehend it with self-introspection. Just as you can conquer anger by understanding it rather than fighting it, similarly, you can be free from attachment by understanding it.

Therefore, if you find attachment to your family, position, social status, wealth, etc., introspect honestly, "What does this attachment drive me to do?" When you witness that these attachments veil your true being, you begin to detach from them. To facilitate this, ask yourself, "For the things I am attached to today, how much attachment should I have next year? Will my detachment increase or decrease by next year?" The more clarity you gain in this matter, the more you will feel detached.

Consistently work on this to make this happen gradually. If you strive for a couple of days to get rid of the attachment completely, you will not reap the desired outcome. It is essential to decide and persistently progress step by step toward detachment and experience the joy of liberation.

> **Essence:** Attachment is the cause of all suffering, while detachment leads us toward joy. Attachment leads to enslavement, while detachment brings freedom. By consciously witnessing attachment, you gradually emerge from the stupor of non-awareness and attain liberation from the captivity of slavery.

41
The Essence of Worldly Love

In ancient times, people used to retreat to the Himalayas to conquer their defilements and tendencies and purify themselves by practicing penance. However, you don't have to travel far; the world around you serves as the practice ground for your spiritual practice.

Question: My husband works in the US, and I used to call him daily. After reflecting on my attachment, I reduced the frequency of my phone calls. My husband asked me, "Why don't you call? Do you want to become a renunciate?" Will I truly renounce the world and become a renunciate by doing so?

Answer: Some people shy away from spirituality for fear of becoming renunciates. But here, you are guided to become a bright householder who practices renunciation while actively engaging in the world. A bright householder expresses love in different ways. Your husband has expressed his love by asking you this question. You, too, can express your love in a different way.

A bright householder couple should love each other and mutually help each other to deepen their love for God. This is not about becoming a renunciate but rather creatively expressing love while living in the world. Your husband is asking you to call him under the pretext of complaints. You can also creatively communicate to him that you will fulfill his wish.

A bright householder transcends conditional love and embodies unconditional love. Otherwise, we often engage in conditional love in the world. When conditions are not met, complaints arise, and such love creates stress.

When there is unconditional love, it gradually transforms into universal love, awakening love and compassion for all living beings. Compassionate love is a divine quality that propels us toward God. When filled with such profound love, we don't have to love consciously; love gets expressed spontaneously.

Remember this pure, divine feeling when conversing with your husband. He will feel better, leading to better results.

> **Essence:** When pure love for yourself and others awakens within you, your relatives will not remain untouched by it. They, too, will experience love through you. You will be transformed from a worldly householder to a bright householder radiating pure love in this world.

42
The Essence of Body Donation

 If you feel good after donating, know that you have donated in the right spirit. Donations driven by obligation, or a mere sense of duty, lack the joy that comes from giving willingly.

Question: Is it appropriate to donate the organs of our body after death?

Answer: First, gain an understanding of the purpose behind donation; then, you can consciously donate anything with ease.

You can make the decision to donate your body parts after death while you are still alive. You need not wait for a specific time for this. If you wish that your body should be put to good use for someone else after your death, you should communicate this intention in writing to the relevant organization.

Most often, people hesitate to donate items because they either think that by donating, they will have less, or they are emotionally attached to those items.

Just imagine if someone steals that item, then what will happen? Consider that you have a beautiful, unused watch in your house.

You think of donating it, yet you are attached to it. Then, one day, the watch is stolen. Won't you feel sad about it? You might think, "Oh! It would have been better if I had donated it to someone instead of it being stolen." In essence, consider donating whatever you intend to without being attached to them.

You may have heard the story of King Harishchandra from the Indian mythology. He selflessly donated his entire kingdom and finally himself to keep his promise to Sage Vishwamitra. Not even for a moment did he harbor any attachment. Hence, he is revered as a great donor.

Many people express their desire to donate but lack the perspective of "donating when they are alive." Everyone is aware of the inevitable truth that one day, upon the demise of their physical body, they will leave everything behind and depart. Despite this, the mind cannot let go of its attachments to these things and this becomes an obstacle in donating. You need to develop this understanding within: "I don't know when my last day on Earth is. Since I have resolved to donate, let me do it at the earliest."

Most people are so strongly attached to the material world comprising of their body, possessions, relationships, and wealth that they find it impossible to donate anything. Some people grieve over the death of their loved ones for their entire life as they cannot let go of their attachment. When a relative embarks on their journey to the afterlife, consider that too as a form of donation and accept their death with a new understanding.

Another aspect you must understand is that whatever you intend to donate should be in good condition. If you are contemplating donating your body, resolve to donate it consciously while you are still alive. Clearly articulate the underlying intention that you are donating it for the welfare of society instead of merely imitating others to put up a show.

In short, when you resolve to donate anything, ensure that you don't have any attachment to it. Don't harbor any doubts in your mind about whether donating your body was the right decision. If you intend to donate your body parts, initiate the process of purifying them through the practice of forgiveness. While you are alive, consistently cleanse every part of your body through forgiveness and keep them healthy. Only then will your donation be worthwhile in a true sense.

Essence: Before donating your body parts, be clear about your perspective behind the donation. While living in this world, do not carry any attachments to worldly things. Then, you will be able to donate anything easily.

PART II

The Pure Essence Beyond The World

43
The Essence of the Eternal Experience

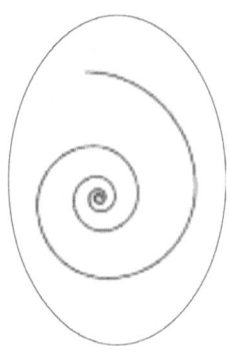

 The sense of living presence is all-pervading, inside the body as well as outside. It is the source of human existence, not the other way round.

Question: What is the meaning of "*Sanaatan*" experience?

Answer: No manmade device or Artificial Intelligence (AI) can ever realize nature's most subtle and profound mystery. The human body is the most capable instrument designed for this purpose.

Whenever anyone has narrated their experiences, they have used words in the language prevalent at that time and place. Since ancient times, the Sanskrit term "*Sanaatan*" has been commonly used in spirituality, which essentially means eternal, perpetual, continuous, constant, forever, etc. However, with the passage of time, it got wrongly associated with religion, rituals, tradition, etc. This has resulted in some people claiming authority over this term while some distancing themselves from it. For example, water, wasser, aqua, l'eau, *paani*, and *jal* are different names of the same substance, but some people prefer or avoid using one over the other.

In such a situation, it is natural to have misunderstandings about the eternal experience that the term Sanaatan originally pointed at. When the term "eternal experience" is associated with religion or tradition, it appears to be exclusively related to certain people. However, it is the same experience that has been attained by enlightened masters like Adi Shankaracharya, Lord Mahavir, the Buddha, Jesus, Prophet Muhammad, or Saint Kabir. This very experience is the experience of beingness, the sense of living presence.

Careful observation shows that we are not our bodies since we can observe our bodies. Whatever is observed is not the observer. Even our thoughts can be observed. Therefore, we are not our thoughts. We are the knower of our thoughts. This knowing continues even in the gap between thoughts.

This deep knowing or consciousness is the eternal essence of life. It is who we truly are. It can be experienced as the feeling of being alive and awake to whatever is happening. This unspoken song of presence is being played constantly; we are that song.

The term "Sanaatan" can be broken down into "Sa + na + tan" which in Hindi means "that which does not pertain to the body." In truth, this eternal experience transcends and pervades our body, mind, intellect, and senses.

Every human body is connected to this eternal experience. Depending on the state of the body and mind, one may or may not realize it. Nevertheless, the experience is ever-present. It is like a child on the mother's lap, whether asleep or awake, always connected with her.

Let us comprehend this profound mystery with an analogy. The eternal experience pervades the illusory world like an ocean. Numerous boats are floating all around this ocean. You, along with other boats, are dwelling in the eternal experience. Other boats come and collide with you one by one. However, not everyone is aware of this experience. Although the eternal experience is ever present, if you are unaware of it, it will still function, but you cannot experience its bliss.

Similarly, one spends their entire life in the eternal experience of consciousness, but due to their lifestyle, tendencies, wrong beliefs, and physical state, they remain bereft of that blissful experience. Hence, despite the inherent presence of the experience of beingness, it is as good as not being present for them as they are unaware of it.

In contemporary language, this eternal experience can be described as "That which exists forever, does not die, or end." It can also be described in simple, light-hearted words without diminishing its meaning or magnificence. It is an ever-new, fresh, and enlivening experience. It is a state of peace and tranquility if you dwell in it with awareness. And if you are disconnected from that experience, you find yourself agitated and distressed.

Those who have not realized this eternal experience live their entire lives as individuals with an ego personality. They yearn for appreciation and validation from others. In doing so, they mistakenly perceive themselves through the lens of others. However, people change, and so do their perspectives and opinions, resulting in an agitated life. In contrast, the eternal experience is permanent within everyone, and everyone can experience it at every moment.

To comprehend the eternal experience fully, its essence must permeate the subconscious mind, which is connected to the universal mind, omnipresent in everyone. As the essence of the eternal experience is realized through more and more human bodies, the highest state of evolution will manifest in the world.

Essence: The answers to all the questions of the universe, solutions to all the puzzles, and the treasure of the eternal experience already exist within each of us. All that is required is to develop an unwavering conviction about it.

44

The Essence of an Egoist Mindset and a Wise Mindset

 *Everything is bestowed on us by God, except our ego, which we have nurtured. Therefore, if we surrender our ego, it can bring about a profound transformation in our life.*

Question: If the ego distinguishes itself from others, does that mean people who accomplished great, distinguished deeds were egoists?

Answer: Great accomplishments can be achieved in two ways:

1. By forgetting the real Self
2. By knowing and being the real Self

When one forgets one's true Self and considers oneself separate from others, it is the true ego. And further, when the true ego considers itself superior to others, it gives rise to a false ego. The desire to stand out and accomplish great achievements and rise above others arises because of the true ego and the false egoistic thoughts. Both types of egos stem from the ignorance of the true Self and the resulting unconscious state of the mind.

On the other hand, those who experience the true Self as the divine consciousness that enlivens everything, for which the body is a medium, and perceive the formless divinity within everyone, engage in great and distinct actions for the welfare of society. This happens due to the awakening of self-conscious awareness.

When one engages in creative endeavors with a higher understanding of this truth, it is not backed by the feeling of doing something unique or distinct from others. They just keep performing the work intuitively, drawing inspiration from within. They have no interest in setting themselves apart from others. Driven by inspiration from within, such creation does not boost the ego.

Great masters have written profound literature for the well-being of humanity, but there was no sense of doer-ship. The thought of taking credit, "I did it," did not arise within them as they had pure wisdom devoid of the ego of being wise. The realization of the experience of the Self, with the help of their pure minds, made them instrumental in achieving such outstanding accomplishments.

If we reflect on the life of the Indian Saint Tulsidas, he struggled like an ordinary man throughout his life while he was also immersed in the service of Lord Rama as an ardent devotee. But, nowhere in his verses, has he mentioned that he accomplished the remarkable feat of composing the "Sri Ramcharitmanas," an epic poetic work based on the Ramayana. Nowhere in his dialogues or couplets did he assert, "I did this."

This illustrates the difference between a true devotee and an egoist. The thoughts of the egoist revolve around "I." They perform their actions accordingly and constantly make a pomp show that they have done it to seek validation and appreciation from others. However, those who perform their actions with a pure and egoless mindset, think about the welfare of everyone. Hence, they are capable of creating something novel and innovative.

> **Essence:** One who refrains from boasting and flaunting their achievements, truly lead an egoless life for the welfare of everyone.

45
The Essence of Self-Experience Beyond the Ego

Serving the ego is the first step toward man's downfall. Serving the Truth beyond the ego is the first step toward man's upliftment.

Question: After listening to the words of wisdom, my mind tends to regard itself knowledgeable and becomes egoistic. What should I do?

Answer: First, let us understand what it means when the mind deems itself knowledgeable. When someone describes a beautiful city to you, your mind creates an imaginary mental picture out of it and believes it to be the truth. Similarly, when the mind receives knowledge of the truth, it tries to understand it intellectually but does not practice it at the level of experience.

Whenever someone talks about that city, you may immediately assert, "I know it." But your acquaintance is merely intellectual. There is a significant difference between envisaging the city and actually visiting it to experience its beauty.

This is akin to taking the required measurements for a house to be constructed, drafting its blueprint, and estimating its construction cost on paper. Without actually going through the experience of building the house, you remain unaware of the potential challenges that may arise during construction. Yet, despite lacking the experience, when someone talks about it, you tend to exaggerate your understanding, claiming, "Yes, I know it, it happens like this, it happens like that," and so on.

The intellect is limited, but the bliss of Self-experience is limitless. However, the mind considers itself knowledgeable and thus loses this bliss. The moment it proclaims, "I know it," it blocks the path to further understanding and experience.

The mind does not like being told that it is wrong. It always safeguards its ego by firmly believing, "I am always right." As a result, it continues to be inert and indolent, always seeking appreciation from others. Hence, it uses the words of wisdom only to justify that it is knowledgeable.

If you are able to comprehend the subtle play of the ego within, you get the opportunity to eliminate it. For this, you can work on the following three steps.

1. **Honest inquiry of the mind:** The mind will logically justify how it is right, but counter it with questions that can eliminate its ego. Those who are honest with themselves immediately understand this process. They work on their thoughts and stop feeding the ego.

   Convince the mind that it cannot gain much by proving itself right. It will only get temporary relief at the cost of permanent happiness. With this conviction, the mind will open to a new experience, and this readiness, in turn, will be the auspicious beginning of its transcendence.

2. **Service of the truth:** When the mind is engaged in serving the truth, many of its limitations and shortcomings come to

light. It realizes how little of the words of wisdom it has truly understood, resulting in the shattering of the ego.

3. **Seek the refuge of an awakened Guru:** The saying, "Iron sharpens iron," may hold good in the external world, but in the inner world, the ego cannot eliminate itself. It is impossible to hold and lift the chair you are seated on. Similarly, the ego cannot break down on its own. Only an awakened Guru can help the disciple in attaining freedom from the ego completely.

Essence: To know something intellectually and experiencing it are two different aspects. Superficial knowledge often feeds the ego, while Self-experience eradicates it.

46
The Essence of Healing Injured Memories

All the material possessions we accumulate during life on Earth are left behind along with our physical bodies. We only carry forward benevolent feelings, the wisdom of the Truth, and positive thoughts in the afterlife. Therefore, live with noble intentions and benevolent thoughts.

Question: Every human body holds some old, injured memories. You have explained that if they remain unhealed during their lifetime, the Universal Self transfers them into new bodies for healing. But how do we know whose injured memories have been implanted within us, causing us so much pain and anxiety?

Answer: Let's understand this with an example. Suppose someone prepares delicious *biryani* and serves it to you lovingly. But as you start relishing it, you find a few tiny stones in the dish. What would you do? Obviously, you would avoid consuming the stones. You would first carefully segregate the stones before savoring the biryani.

Further, you can even learn to make a bridge out of the stones, i.e., turn the negative situation into an opportunity to raise your level of consciousness. No need to find or blame the person who prepared the biryani. Instead, strive to see that you remove all the stones from the biryani before passing it on to others if it needs to be served.

In a similar vein, there is no need to find or blame the individuals whose injured memories may have been implanted within you. If at all injured memories within you are to be transferred to any other body after the death of your body, you must heal and purify them during your lifetime on earth. For this, offer prayers, practice forgiveness, nurture benevolent feelings for all, wish for the well-being of all, and lead an impersonal life on earth.

You may find it challenging to put all this into practice initially, but maintaining a noble and clear intention will make it easier. If you firmly resolve, "I must heal all my injured memories," all obstacles will be cleared, and with consistent practice, you will see a positive transformation in your life. Incorporate practices such as listening to discourses on the truth, introspection, journaling, and meditation as part of your daily routine. Then, gradually, this practice will become an integral part of your nature.

You may ask, "Why do I need to undertake all these activities?" Let's understand it with an example. You clean your house every morning. However, you find it unclean the next day, so you clean it again. Why do you repeat the cleaning process every day? Because one-time cleaning does not help, the house becomes dirty every now and then. When you see the house spick and span, you won't tolerate even a small speck. Similarly, when you become aware of your injured memories and take steps to heal them, you will experience inner solace. Thereafter, the moment you will feel uncomfortable within, you will want to heal the negative, hurtful feeling immediately to regain that solace.

Essence: Do not continue to drudge through life with injured memories and pass them on to others. Instead, consistently cleanse yourself within with the help of spiritual practices like listening to the discourses of truth, introspection, offering prayer, journaling, and meditation. As your level of consciousness rises, healing will happen.

47
The Essence of the Divine Form

 God is the seed, and His power is the tree. The potential of an entire forest exists within that one seed. The entire world is a manifestation of God's potential. Thus, Oneness is the essence of the diversity and plurality of the vast cosmos.

Question: I keep hearing that we are the divine manifestation of God. Please explain this.

Answer: Consider the waves rising in the ocean. Are they distinct entities or an integral part of the ocean? They are, indeed, part of the ocean. Now, imagine a wave rising so high that it touches the sky or the Sun. Then what would happen? It would seem as if the entire ocean has touched the sky or the Sun through the medium of that wave.

Whether you call the wave a miniature form of the ocean or the ocean as the expanded form of the wave, they are the same. The wave rising in the ocean is not separate from the ocean; it is a manifestation of the ocean in a different form. Every wave rising from the ocean has its own unique form. Hence, it appears distinct. Some waves are small, while others are large.

If a wave were to realize that it is none other than the ocean itself, it would be grateful to the ocean. It would thank the ocean because it has understood that it is the ocean, and this understanding has also been bestowed by the ocean itself. Just as every part of the ocean, including the wave, is the ocean itself, every part of God, whether minuscule or gigantic, is inherently God itself!

This analogy of the wave-in-the-ocean conveys the fundamental concept. However, words have their own limitations. Many times, it is not possible to communicate the highest wisdom completely using the medium of worldly language. When you connect with the Source, the profound mysteries beyond words are revealed. Connecting with the Source implies realizing the experience of the true Self, being immersed in the experience of the divine eternal consciousness.

Divine wisdom cannot be explained precisely in words, but it can be surely pointed at through words, stories, examples, analogies, indications, symbols, and signs. True transformation occurs in life only when the understanding of the ultimate truth is fully imbibed at the level of experience. Even if such transformation is not immediately evident, persist in the pursuit of truth without getting stuck at the hurdles or pitfalls on the journey. Proceed with whatever you have understood so far. It may take time, but the mystery will eventually unfold on its own.

> **Essence:** God exists in every infinitesimal part of the world. Divine Consciousness is inherent in every manifestation of nature, be it objects, flora, fauna, or all living beings. Conversely, each of us is a form of God, a part of God.

48
The Essence of Divine Wisdom

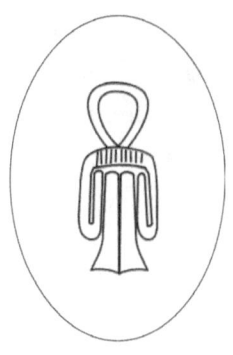

Those who realized the living essence within them called it "the Supreme silence." Supreme silence cannot be comprehended by the intellect as it transcends the intellect. Hence, it has been also called "Leela - the Divine play" or "Divine Grace."

Question: God has created a beautiful and self-perpetuating toy in the form of a human being, which is indeed a great wonder! What must have God thought or intended while creating it, and what form did God embody to manifest this auspicious thought? What kind of intellect did He employ to conceive such a profound creation?

Answer: Whenever people talk about God, they often envision God in the human form. They assume God to be like them. As they are constantly engaged in thinking, they consider that God must have had some similar process of thinking and planning before creating man. However, language came into existence only after the world was created. Hence, due to the constraint of language, it is said, "God created." But ponder this: How can something that existed before the birth of language be expressed in terms of the language that evolved only after the creation of the world?

God always already exists even before the creation of time and space. We speak in a language that often refers to the past, present, or future, that has come into existence after the creation of time. However, when the world did not exist, the measure of time did not exist either. Time appeared after the world came into existence, and using the measure of time, we want to know when the world was created. How long was God alone before creating the world?

We want an answer about what existed before time, based on the measure of time itself! However, our language is inadequate to describe the timeless essence that existed before time. Hence, we find those answers illogical.

To envision God in the human form is an attempt to comprehend the experience of God, the true Self. If we use examples of formless elements like nature, the sky, or the ocean to refer to God, people cannot understand because these formless elements lack a tangible shape or a form that can be easily grasped. So, having committed the mistake of trying to understand God in some tangible form, questions arise within people, "How did God think of creating man? How did God do it?"

Answers to these questions are found in the first verse of the fourth chapter of the Bhagavad Gita, where Lord Krishna states, "I imparted this wisdom to the Sun first." Here, Lord Krishna is not referring to his physical form as "I" but rather the Pure Consciousness that existed prior to all creation.

Understand it this way. Self-realization happens through a body-mind mechanism. The body glorifies and describes the Self as Consciousness, the experience of existence, the eternal presence, or aliveness. Although the Self is beyond words, the body adores the experience of the Self in words. The body can speak only because of the presence of the Self within. So then, what is essentially happening? The Self is communicating through the body and imparting wisdom to itself as the listener. The Self, which is beyond words, speaks through the body using words, and the Self alone listens to it first. It is knowing about itself through its own body-mind mechanism. The Creator is knowing Himself through His creation by using the medium of words.

However, "The Sun was given the knowledge first" seems illogical because the Sun is not a human being capable of receiving knowledge. Through this statement, Lord Krishna wants to convey, "I gave the knowledge to myself first." Essentially, the Self gave this knowledge to itself first, serving as the ultimate source of wisdom. After that, the knowledge was given to humanity. However, the sentence, "I gave this knowledge to myself first," leads to confusion, and people fail to understand it.

The common misconception is that God donned a human form first and then, after a lot of contemplation, created the world. Our logical mind assumes that God needs to think to create; without thinking, He cannot create. However, God is the ultimate Source, beyond words and form. God transcends the framework of language. Hence the answer to the question, which body did God don to create the world, is, "That body which God donned to impart wisdom to Himself." Only after God received the wisdom about Himself did the entire series of forms and phenomena begin to unfold.

> **Essence:** Describing God's functioning through worldly language is challenging because language is a human creation. Hence, do not conceptualize God in terms of thoughts or behavior as you would envisage yourself. God is the supreme all-pervading energy that creates and sustains the entire world.

49
The Essence of Polytheism

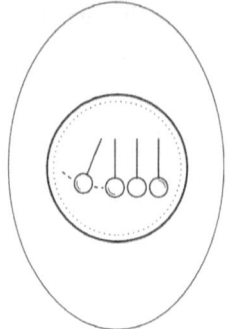

In an attempt to imagine and conceptualize the experience of the true Self, various faiths and religions have emerged around the world. However, the true Self is the pure unmanifest essence, transcending perception, without blemish, neither an image nor an imagination.

Question: People of different religions worship different Gods. And in the case of polytheist religions like Hinduism, several Gods are venerated in the same religion. What is the purpose behind this?

Answer: Let's understand this in four steps:

1. With the current global population being eight billion, it can be said that there are eight billion Gods. It can also be said that God created us, and we conceived our own Gods.

2. Each religion conceived God according to their specific beliefs because people harbored different kinds of fear. The enlightened souls observed the troubles and vulnerabilities faced by people. They sensed that people were incapable of asking the right questions and receiving the right answers. Illogical truths were beyond their understanding.

Therefore, according to the beliefs and needs of those times and those communities, to alleviate fears and instill faith in divinity, enlightened saints conceived Gods and explained certain aspects about those Gods to the masses. This was essential to prevent people from getting caught up in the endless cycle of questions and answers and direct their focus to the perception of the truth.

3. Different Gods were envisioned to instill devotion and elevate the masses to a higher level of consciousness. However, with time, people forgot the original purpose and got consumed by their egos, holding the belief that "I know everything."

4. While speaking of the Gods, Lord Krishna states, "I am the One who expresses through all the Gods." This means that the Source is one and the same across all religions. However, people have forgotten or become oblivious of the Source, started believing in multiple Gods, and entangled in various rituals to appease those Gods.

In India, people pray to different deities for different purposes. For example, they pray to a certain deity for rain or to another to reduce excessive rainfall. They pray to a particular Goddess for wealth, another for knowledge, and so on.

But the situation is now changing. People are becoming more aware. They are receiving the highest wisdom and realizing its importance. Hence, harness this wisdom to the best of your ability. When you delve into the true essence of religion and decode the actual meaning of these deities, all doubts and questions about God will disappear.

Essence: There were several reasons for having so many Gods. However, every religion fundamentally believes that the Source is One, the true Self. Experience the sense of living presence within. When you realize this experience of the true Self, all your questions will dissolve.

50
The Essence of Earthly Life

One who knows the truth that "Earth is a training school" does not waste one's precious moments of life. They learn their vital life lessons from every incident and live a blossomed life.

Question: It is said that we have come on Earth donning this body to accomplish a specific purpose. Where have we come from? Do we belong to some other place beyond Earth? Where do we exist when we are not on Earth?

Answer: When you firmly believe that "God alone exists," the concept of "coming from somewhere" or "going elsewhere" doesn't hold. "Coming from somewhere" implies that God wasn't already here. "Going elsewhere" implies that God isn't already present there. As God is all-pervading, there is nowhere to come from and nowhere to go. Such words are used due to the constraints of language.

In simple language, God is experiencing Himself through every individual body. New bodies are created; however, they are made up of the same five fundamental elements of nature: Earth, water, fire, air, and ether. It is like constructing a new building with the material used for the old building. Regardless of how many bodies come into existence and become extinct, they are made up of these five fundamental elements, and the Consciousness, the true Self, alone experiences itself through all of them. The experiences gathered by the Self through a particular body are available in the form of memories. The Self re-uses memories gathered from one human lifetime by planting them in further bodies to evolve progressively.

For example, you would have heard of child prodigies who exhibit remarkable skills early in their childhood. There are three-year-olds who play the piano skillfully, and kindergarten children who solve complex mathematical problems effortlessly. This shows how the Self reuses memories of experiences from previous bodies.

The inherent nature of the Self is to grow and evolve. Growth is on the material plane of existence, and evolution on the spiritual plane. The Self achieves this by re-using memories gathered from different bodies after their physical death and implanting them in further bodies. The Self explores its boundless potential through this journey of progressive evolution, ultimately, leading to Self-realization, and expression of its divine qualities.

Essentially, all memories are available to the Self, just as all the websites are available on the internet. Whatever link you click on, the corresponding website opens. Similarly, those memories that are implanted in a particular body, operate through that body. The body comes into existence on Earth and becomes extinct here itself, while memories emanate from the ocean of the Self. Hence, it is said, "We come on Earth."

Essence: Every time the Self dons a body, it is to learn some lessons, progress, and evolve. However, the body's limitations and external factors affect it in such a manner that its learning of the necessary lessons remains incomplete. This happens naturally. As Consciousness evolves, it breaks free from this cycle.

51

The Essence of Progress and Transcendence

 *Beliefs and misconceptions limit human progress; bringing them to light fosters transcendence.*

Question: What is the difference between progress and transcendence?

Answer: Progress relates to advancements in the external world. Everyone aspires to progress to realize their utmost potential. They work according to their abilities so that their latent potential, skills, and qualities find a ground to flourish fully. For that, they train themselves in various fields. Then, they choose an occupation where they get the opportunity to express and enhance their talents and qualities, thus allowing them to excel in their field.

Transcendence relates to growth in our inner world, aimed at attaining our ultimate purpose on earth, realizing our true Self, stabilizing in the state of supreme bliss, and expressing divine qualities of the true Self.

Our mission on Earth is accomplished when we train the mind to be steadfast, obedient, untainted, and loving. With this training, the mind learns to remain unshakable in the face of challenging situations, negative thoughts, or moments of sorrow or disappointment. We win over the mind by transcending it, after which the mind does not make us unhappy. Instead, by conversing with the mind, we learn the art of making the mind devoted and contented.

Often, people ask, "What should we do in such a situation? How do we navigate through negativity?" In reality, the primary goal of every human being is to be free from their sorrows. In this context, progress entails attaining a deeper understanding of suffering and adopting practices that alleviate disappointment and worries.

In the pursuit of transcendence, when one works on the triad of Truth—listening to the Truth, service of the Truth, and devotion to the Truth—they encounter numerous opportunities in the garb of trivial situations where their mind falters. This newfound and advancing awareness prompts them to train their mind to remain happy and steadfast amid these situations.

When one ascends to the pinnacle of transcendental growth, one attains the highest evolved state, where there is no separation from the Self. Separation from our true essence is the root cause of sorrow. The Self continually urges us to advance toward the highly evolved state. By causing a feeling of sorrow, the Self reminds us to prioritize our transcendence.

Therefore, whenever you experience sorrow, perceive it as a reminder from the Self, "I am at the highest level that you aspire to reach. I await here, but you aren't rising to the occasion. Hence, I have sent this feeling of sorrow as a gift to motivate you to advance and not remain stuck. Come here, where I am now, which is your original home." This is transcendence, which eliminates the separation between the Self and the individual, after which benevolent prayers arise for the well-being of the entire world. In this state, only bliss prevails, and personal worries cease to exist.

Essence: When we progress on the spiritual plane, our journey toward the Truth unfolds, away from worldly distractions, and the mind dwells in lasting happiness. This is transcendental growth. Everyone must strive to advance from progress toward transcendence.

52
The Essence of Sleep

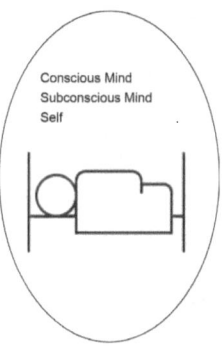

Under the influence of the knowledge of the Self, the ego falls, the illusion vanishes, and the divine consciousness manifests in the human body. This state is referred to as the experience of the true Self, the transcendental experience wherein the Self is aware of itself.

Question: Exactly who sleeps at night - the physical body, the conscious mind, the subconscious mind, the brain, or consciousness itself?

Answer: The answer depends on your understanding of sleep. The conscious mind sleeps during the night, and consciousness sleeps during the day. The conscious and subconscious minds are aspects of the same mind, but often functionally distinguished for clarity. The body, mind, and intellect serve as tools of the Self, and the Self uses them.

The intellect guides our thoughts, yet the mind believes, "I am doing everything." The conscious mind that holds this belief, sleeps during the night so our thoughts calm down. However, upon waking up, the incessant stream of thoughts resumes. So, it is the stream of thoughts that goes to sleep, and the stream of thoughts that wakes up.

One who becomes engrossed in thoughts forgets their true being, the Self. Thoughts dominate in the waking hours and consciousness recedes to the dark, being unaware of itself. Therefore, it is said that consciousness sleeps during the day. The state of awakening of the Self is called Enlightenment. Until this state is attained, the Self remains asleep during the day.

This is a profound point. Let us understand it with an example. Imagine a person manning the railway inquiry counter. When they feel drowsy, they put up a "Closed" signboard and nap. Similarly, by listening to someone's conversation, one can discern whether the Self is asleep or awakened within that body. If they feel sad in a situation, it indicates that the Self within them is asleep. And if you feel unhappy about it, it means the Self within you is also in a state of slumber.

If the Self is awakened within you, instead of feeling unhappy, you will happily strive to awaken the Self within others through your conscious presence. With this understanding, reflect on your entire life: How have you been living life? What are the underlying beliefs and assumptions that guide your thoughts? What have you assumed yourself to be, based on which thoughts arise – the body, mind, intellect, or the Self? Honestly answer these questions and realize the Truth.

> **Essence:** The body, mind, and intellect serve as tools for the Self. When used appropriately, they can help us dwell in the awakened state, the enlightened state, wherein the Self remains aware of its essential nature and expresses its divine qualities from that self-aware awareness.

53

The Essence of the Self

That which remains after all the wrong tendencies of the mind are eliminated is the true Essence, the Self, the Living Presence, the Source. Its mere presence spreads love, joy, and peace in human life.

Question: How can I know the true Self?

Answer: Who is the "I" that wants to know the Self? The real knower is the Self itself. The mind wants to know the Self, but it is incapable of this. The Self is the unknowable experiencer that can be experienced only by being it; not by standing apart from it. The Self constantly knows the mind too; however, the mind cannot know the Self who is knowing everything.

Let us understand this with the concept of the knower-known-knowing.

The "knower" is the subject who knows, the "known" is the object being known, and "knowing" is the act of the subject knowing the object. Here, the mind assumes itself as the knower and assumes that "I am knowing." However, the mind is also being known. And the act of knowing is also being known. The Self makes a sandwich out of the knower, known, and knowing, and uses this sandwich as a medium to experience itself, a mirror to behold itself.

The Self exists both inside and outside the body. Due to the limitations of language, words such as "inside" and "outside" are being used to express this. But, in truth, the Self is beyond both inside and outside as it pervades all that is.

The Self cannot be known by standing separately. It can be experienced only by being it. By engaging in unceasing spiritual practice, this will become possible.

> **Essence:** By "being" the knower, witness the known and the process of knowing. The Self is the true essence, the true being. The essence of all spiritual practices, like listening to the knowledge of the truth, meditation, and introspection, is to experience the Self. The Self is always present as a witness to this spiritual practice through which it is the Self alone, that is attempting to experience itself.

54
The Essence of Spiritual Knowledge

 Negative thoughts arise from an ignorant mind, fueled by fears. To overcome their impact, question the validity of each negative thought through introspection.

Question: I have heard that too much meditation can cause physical pain. What happens in these spiritual retreats? Why are they necessary? Are there any negative effects of these retreats?

Answer: In the pursuit of profound wisdom, guidance unfolds gradually. A series of progressive retreats has been established to facilitate this journey. Seekers undergo step-by-step preparation, enhancing their understanding in a step-by-step manner. This is referred to as the "System for Wisdom" at Tej Gyan Foundation.

As your understanding deepens, subsequent retreats provide knowledge at the next level. There is no need to dwell on labels like discomforts, pains, or side effects, and there is no need to fear them either.

Consider the analogy of school education. First, you grasp the syllabus of Class One. Subsequently, you advance to Class Two, followed by sequential progression through Classes Three, Four, and so forth. This incremental approach ensures step-by-step progress. You are not sent to Class Ten directly.

The next question is, "Is there a need to attend further retreats?" With time, this will be clear to you. Meanwhile, persist in listening to discourses and refining your capacity to absorb knowledge. Gradually, you will realize that you are elevating your readiness and receptivity to receive higher wisdom. You will also cultivate the discernment to navigate the right path and foster conviction in the understanding in which you need to be established, within yourself.

The discourses guide you to dwell in the self-aware consciousness, the experience of the true Self. However, as the experience of the gross body is predominant, understanding the subtler aspects takes time. Moreover, the events in your daily life exert a strong influence, leading you to prioritize your personal and your loved ones' needs. However, by adhering to the system for wisdom, these challenges will be gradually resolved. Knowledge is imparted here only when you are prepared, ensuring it doesn't lead to confusion or dilemma.

Many seekers embark on their spiritual journey by emphasizing practices related to the physical body, striving to attain occult powers. They find it difficult to meditate for long hours, but they put their bodies through arduous and strenuous practices with the desire to achieve extraordinary powers. On that path, their ego gets boosted. But here, the emphasis is not on acquiring such powers in the physical or psychic realms. Instead, the focus lies on experiencing the true Self beyond all these dimensions – an ordinary and fundamental realization of one's true essence. The goal is to dissolve the ego rather than bolster it. As you advance, you will notice the gradual dissolution of the ego within; bit by bit, it begins to melt away.

Hence, proceed without fear or presumptions, contemplating the knowledge imparted. You will be guided by your own experience and insights, and you will find answers to all your questions emerging from within.

> **Essence**: Spirituality is the art of being life. Prior to embarking on spiritual practices or meditation, knowledge is imparted to make you aware and prepared. When you encounter something entirely new and transcendent, there is no need to fear or become stuck. You can then fearlessly advance on the path of Truth.

55

The Essence of Worthiness to Attain the Truth

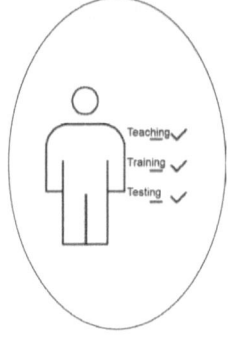

If one is uncertain about what to ask for and not capable enough to safeguard what one receives, one remains unhappy and dissatisfied even after receiving it. Hence, enhance your understanding and eligibility to receive and safeguard it before asking for it.

Question: Can I ever become eligible to attain the Truth?

Answer: Everyone can become eligible to attain the Truth. The mere fact of being born human indicates the inherent eligibility for receiving the nectar of the Truth. However, without proper training to receive it, the nectar of the Truth can never reach you; and even if it does reach you, you will lose it.

Nature does not discriminate or play favorites. Everyone has the potential to attain the Truth, but their bodies may not be adequately prepared to receive it. Therefore, the first step involves preparing and readying the mind and body through teaching, training, and testing.

When being trained in this manner, it is natural for one to think, "I am asking for something, yet receiving something else." However, they are unaware they are being prepared according to their desires. How the training gets scripted into your journey of attaining the Truth is in the unseen. It is your prayer, but on this path, you may find that whatever manifests may not match with what you have asked for. Hence, you might feel you are not receiving what you prayed for.

In truth, whatever you receive is the result of your karma and the power of your prayers. If you aspire to attain the Truth, you need to be prepared for it to some extent in advance.

Imagine you are serving a pure and wholesome meal, and somebody extends a dirty plate toward you, requesting you to serve them the food. Would you agree to serve them the food on that dirty plate? You would tell them, "Clean the dish first. Otherwise, the food will lose its essence. It will also become unhygienic and unsuitable for consumption."

Similarly, before imparting wisdom, your mind is being made to undergo purification. Impurities like vices, beliefs, tendencies, and injured memories are eliminated from your body-mind so that it becomes pure and deserving to receive wisdom.

Essence: Everyone has the potential to attain the Truth, but it is essential to evaluate your own worthiness. Are your mind and body pure and clean? If not, it needs to undergo purification with the knowledge of the Truth. Subsequently, the experience of the Self will be revealed within it.

56

The Essence of the Potential of the Human Body

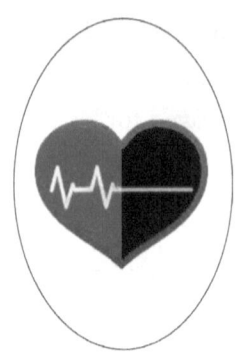

Only humans have the ability to think, reason, understand, learn, and make decisions. By leveraging these abilities and augmenting their capabilities, they can attain the goal of the human body.

Question: Can ardent yogis or other accomplished spiritual practitioners determine the time of their demise?

Answer: Not only yogis, even you have the potential to accomplish this. It is an inherent potential of the human body. However, once you make this decision, you must shoulder the responsibility for the ensuing consequences.

There are people in the world who live for a hundred to hundred and fifty years. In ignorance, people often yearn for a prolonged life, but as old age sets in, the desire for death emerges. These are contradicting prayers—on one hand, they want to live, and on the other hand, they also wish to die. When they confront any troublesome situation, they begin to think, "What is the purpose of living now? Why can't I just die?"

Every human being has the power to determine the time of their death, but for that, they need to raise their level of consciousness. If you desire to live a long life, your purpose of living must be just as strong, and you must also have an understanding of Part Two – life after death. Many people perceive a long life to be a successful life. However, this is only half of their earthly life, known as Part One. They can live a long life with a higher consciousness wherein they remain aware and question themselves, "What is the real purpose behind the desire for a long life?"

If you wish for a prolonged life driven by mundane activities, like eating, sleeping, sitting, and idling away time in worthless pursuits, you may ultimately find this objective meaningless.

For some people, choosing to live a short life is the right decision. However, one can make such decisions only after attaining the experience of the Self and operating from heightened consciousness. A notable example is Saint Dnyaneshwar, who, after attaining Enlightenment, chose to undertake a timeless state of meditation, *Samadhi*, at a very young age. Otherwise, in ignorance, one may aspire to live a long life only to find oneself leading a life marred by sorrow and continual suffering. Then, such a prolonged life serves no purpose. With wisdom, even a short life can suffice to fulfill one's purpose on earth, as demonstrated by masters like Jesus Christ and Swami Vivekananda, who led short yet profoundly meaningful lives.

Therefore, you can also determine the time of your death, provided you are clear about your purpose. To achieve this, first gain the knowledge of Truth, elevate your consciousness; then accept and allow whatever happens afterward.

Essence: Every person has the power to determine the time of their death, provided the underlying purpose is clear. Regardless of whether life is long or short, it must be meaningful.

57
The Essence of Breath as a Reminder

 Beyond the limits of mere recitation of names or ritualistic rosaries, the practice of conscious chanting has the profound purpose of remembering our divine essence and being deeply aware of it. The fulfillment of chanting lies in the experience of the divine essence.

Question: If our breath serves as a bridge between our body and the Self, how can we make the breath a reminder to dwell in the experience of the Self?

Answer: Our breath is evidence of our being alive. This inherent arrangement of nature has two advantages.

1. It provides vital life force and energy.
2. If directed appropriately, it can serve as a powerful reminder for us.

In spirituality, breath is a potent reminder to understand whether every breath being expended is wasted or used wisely. If it is happening unconsciously, it is being wasted. It is being used merely to keep the body alive. It serves no other purpose.

Countless thoughts run endlessly in our mind, entangling us in the memories of the past or plans for the future. As a result, we do not truly remain in the present. However, the breath is the most effective tool for being in the present. As soon as we focus on our breath and observe its inhalation and exhalation, the thoughts in the mind begin to diminish. Hence, first, the breath should be used to bring ourselves into the present and then engage in meditation.

Once we are in the present, we must observe what captivates our interest, what entangles us back into the illusory world, the *Maya*, or connects us to the Self by going beyond the breath. Therefore, to facilitate this process, chanting has been combined with breathing, so that, instead of entangling ourselves in the illusory world, we connect with the Self. A chosen word is used for chanting to remind us of the Truth, the Self.

Our breath can be deep or shallow, ongoing or paused, slow or rapid. But we must be determined that "However be the breath, it will only engage in reminding me of the name," which means that whatever name we have given the Truth, we will keep recalling it.

For example, even before Lord Rama was born, His guru, Sage Vasishtha had named the experience of the Truth, "Rama." He would chant the word "Rama" to remind himself of Self-experience. The newborn prince of Ayodhya was named Rama at the suggestion of the sage.

We must develop the habit of divine remembrance. We can develop the habit of observing our breath when we are seated in meditation, acknowledging its entry and exit. With this, we associate the remembrance of the divine essence. We remember the Truth as the sense of our living presence.

We inculcate the habit of moving to the experience of the Self whenever words like the Presence, Om, God, Allah, or Rama are uttered. This habit is reinforced through repetition. Then, we can even practice divine remembrance while sleeping. If someone questions us in our sleep, and the answer to it is that chosen name, we will remember and chant it in sleep too. Although the body is asleep, we will mention that name. This way, our breath can help us anchor. We can treat it as a rosary of breaths and take time to practice. Until we become proficient in it, we can take the help of external rosaries. Whether an external rosary or a rosary of breaths, their purpose is the same: to ensure that none of our breaths go in vain, and it keeps us connected to the Self.

The pace of our breath keeps changing. Hence, with awareness, we must sit down and study the pace of our breath so that even when we are not conscious, we become aware of the changes in the pace of our breath. Our breath always goes on wherever we are, and it keeps informing us about the state of our mind. We may have noticed that when we are angry, the pace of our breath increases, and when we are at peace, it remains steady. Therefore, we can take double advantage of our breath: as a reminder as well as to know the state of our mind.

> **Essence**: Several breathing exercises have been devised to maintain our physical and mental health. This means that our breath is energy, and its pace reflects our mental state. When we observe our breath as a witnesser, we stay in the present and remain connected with the Self every moment. This serves as a reminder of the Truth.

58
The Essence of Detached Action

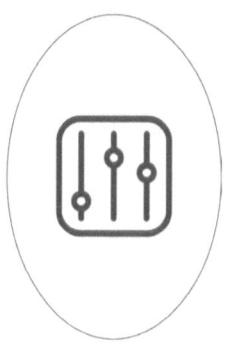

You can receive all that you aspire for in life, provided you are detached from the fruit of action. In other words, you do not get stuck in the outcome and are passionate and focused on your actions, fulfilling your responsibilities.

Question: How can I determine my level of spiritual growth? How can I assess how close I have reached to Self-realization?

Answer: The litmus test for true growth is our internal feeling of contentment. When we savor a hearty meal, our satisfaction is the unmistakable indicator that our stomach is full. No amount of insistence can sway us to consume more, and we say, "Enough! My stomach is full; I don't need any more." What tells us that our stomach is full, that we are satisfied? Our inner feeling of satisfaction tells us. Our craving stops. It is the same with Self-realization.

Your question is on your current level of spiritual progress, and how close you are to Self-realization. The very thought, "How close am I?" reveals an attachment to the outcome. In this journey, shedding this attachment is crucial. Only by freeing yourself from the anticipation of the fruit of spiritual practice can you attain stillness, becoming keenly aware of your unfolding inner experience, about how you are feeling deep within.

Hence, regardless of whether the expected result materializes or not, consistently ask yourself, "How deeply am I engaged in my actions? Am I genuinely enjoying whatever I am experimenting with?" Take inspiration from Thomas Edison, the inventive mind behind the electric bulb. He persevered without knowing when his creation would illuminate. Even when his laboratory was razed down in a fire, instead of succumbing to disappointment, he seized the opportunity to passionately recommence his research.

Similarly, persist in your efforts without worrying about the outcome. The quality of your actions is enhanced when you shift your attention away from the result. Entrust the results to prayer, jot them down in your diary, and allow nature to orchestrate its course. Just as nature has been arranging things so far, it will continue to make provisions for the future.

Imagine preparing a meal; you gather all the ingredients, joyfully start cooking, and hum along as you work. You focus solely on the cooking process, free from concerns about the final dish. In this state, the resulting meal is bound to be delightful, pleasing those who have the meal.

Conversely, imagine cooking while constantly fretting, "Will the food be ready on time? Will the guests appreciate it? I hope I've got all the ingredients, especially the salt, just right." In such an anxious state, there's a chance the salt might be excessive, a vessel could fall, or something might burn. With these worries, the joy of cooking diminishes as we are burdened by concerns like, "How can I do all this? I hope I don't make a mistake."

Similarly, when you get into the spiritual practice, be assured. Remind yourself to stay detached from the outcome by affirming, "Let me enjoy the journey. Let me be mindful of whatever unfolds around and within me. This journey, for me, is the destination in its own right!"

Essence: Detach yourself from the result of your efforts, embracing the assurance that, "However, whenever, wherever it unfolds; I will realize it, feel it, and be liberated." With this attitude, the wondrous realization will unfold naturally and spontaneously. Until then, relish the joy of your actions.

59

The Essence of Spiritual Practice, Liberation, and Rebirth

 God has bestowed upon us the gift of human life. The key question is, "Are we giving ourselves the gift of enhancing the quality of this life?"

Question: There is a prevalent belief that if we don't attain liberation despite performing intense spiritual practice, we are reborn into an affluent family. Please guide me on this.

Answer: The answer is related to memories. The memories of countless past lives are stored within the collective subconscious. Rebirth is nothing but the implanting of some of these memories in a new body where it receives a conducive environment to progress to the next level of spiritual practice.

To facilitate this, they need to be surrounded by people treading on the path of spiritual practice. If such a supportive environment is available, their possibility of advancing further increases. It is not entirely true that they are reborn only in wealthy families. This belief came into existence because affluent people often have more resources available for spiritual upliftment. However, we often equate resources with wealth.

A conducive environment to progress on the path of spiritual practice can be found even in poor families. Numerous saints came from poor, impoverished families. And yet, they attained Self-realization. Therefore, do not assess this solely based on wealth.

Despite pursuing spiritual practices, if liberation is not attained, then those memories are implanted into bodies provided with favorable conditions for spiritual growth.

Those who harbor love for the Truth and follow the path of spiritual practice, and whose parents also tread the same path, find it inherently supportive. This becomes a motivation for them to progress further on the path of spiritual practice.

> **Essence:** If liberation is not attained despite a lifetime of spiritual practice, the memories of these spiritual seekers are transferred to bodies that can find the path to advance in their spiritual journey. Hence, instead of believing in hearsay beliefs, it is crucial to stay steadfast and persevere on the path of spiritual practice.

60
The Essence of Devotion, Quest, and Surrender

 *It is easier to become someone through effort, but it takes complete surrender to let go of all the efforts to become "nothing."*

Question: Which one is better – a devotee's divine devotion or a seeker's intense quest? How can I inculcate the quality of complete surrender to nurture a divine devotion?

Answer: When ice melts, it takes the form of water. When heated, water transforms into vapor, dispersing into space. This depicts the journey of ice from "the form to the formless."

Similarly, a devotee also undergoes various stages in their journey: seeking, devotion, and complete surrender. No stage is right or wrong, better or less better here; each stage is perfect in its own right.

A seeker of the Truth has questions arising in their mind, and answers to those questions also serve as guidance for others. Hence, the stage of the seeker has its importance.

On the other hand, a devotee is immersed in the divine bliss of devotion and serves as a source of inspiration for everyone.

Therefore, it is not important whether you are progressing on your spiritual quest as a seeker or immersing yourself in divine devotion as a devotee. What truly matters is that whatever be your present state, you should continue to receive the impetus to progress and keep preparing yourself for the future stages of the journey. This is a journey of passing through every stage toward the formless truth. By consistently moving ahead without getting entangled in the fixations of forms and rituals, you reach the next stage. The terms like devotee and seeker are used for convenience, and there is no need to get stuck in them.

In the discourses at Tej Gyan Foundation, when everyone is addressed as "Dear Seekers," it is meant to address different people in their varied stages on the journey. Each seeker understands the guru's message based on their present state. Therefore, remain immersed in the feeling of complete surrender and enjoy this journey from ice to water, water to vapor, vapor to space, and finally, the merger into the divine space that encompasses all. The paths may vary, but the destination is the same. Whichever path you take, you will reach the same destination.

Be it devotion or seeking, ultimately, only the state of complete surrender ensues. Initially, one considers oneself separate from others and begins their quest. Gradually, as understanding deepens, complete surrender naturally unfolds at the highest state.

Essence: In the journey of the Truth, the path or stage is not as important as ensuring that you do not get stuck anywhere on your path, that you do not get entangled in rituals or beliefs or get trapped in the egoistic notion that "My path is the best." Instead, keep progressing until you reach the state of complete surrender.

61
The Essence of The Level of Spiritual Progress

When a devotee merges in the experience of oneness with the divine essence at the core of their heart, surrendering the egoic "I," they remain absorbed in supreme consciousness. Then, at every moment, they deeply feel and honor the presence of that all-pervading consciousness everywhere.

Question: You had once said in a discourse that when devotion awakens and crosses the threshold of 51%, the further journey becomes effortless. But how can I ascertain whether my level of devotion has indeed reached 51%?

Answer: There is no greater yardstick than self-experience itself. Once devotion touches the 51% threshold, progress to the next level becomes spontaneous, and external efforts cease. At that juncture, intellectual understanding is not required; it will be your inherent experience.

Initially, you observe as a mindful witness. You consciously make all efforts with the firm intention, "All my actions should be performed with awareness." With awareness, you will realize when you reach 51%, nothing can then impede your progress. Until you recognize this, you strive to experience the self-witnessing presence. While witnessing everything in the external world, you begin to witness the knower of everything. Advancing further, when all the efforts to witness the external world are given up, you shift into Self-witnessing – witnessing of the Self. This marks the transition from being a mere witness of the body-mind and external world to Self-witnessing.

Over time, you go through different states. For example, you observe your body as healthy or sick, tired or fresh, and stressed or peaceful. In every situation, you observe being a witness. When you stumble upon the realization that the knower is being known without any effort, you will be amazed. No one else can convey this; this has to be experienced and recognized all by yourself.

After the threshold of 51% devotion is crossed, numerous layers of conditioning shrouding the body-mind mirror automatically begin to dissolve. Here, your body-mind mechanism is likened to a mirror that is instrumental in experiencing the experiencer through experience. You can see everything clearly without any extra effort. Now, while you look at the mirror, you do not perceive the mirror; instead, you behold that for which the mirror is a reflective medium. And suddenly, you exclaim, "Now, knowing is happening; experiencing is going on!" No separate entity remains to know the knower; it is just the Self, where the subject is no longer distinct from the object of experience. The Self alone is being known externally and internally. Beingness is happening. It happens innately and effortlessly as there is no "checker" mind to judge or check who is experiencing or what is being experienced. When such moments arise, know that the 51% threshold has been attained.

Thereafter, further layers of conditioning will naturally rise and dissolve in due course. But there will be no anxiety about whether or when the level will reach 100% because you are already free from such concerning thoughts. When this state is attained, you naturally recognize it through insight. There are no external symptoms to indicate this state.

Even after reaching this stage, some tendencies may persist within you, but their power begins to diminish, as though someone is clearing them. Subsequently, you will observe that you no longer linger in sorrow as much as before and are less entangled in your tendencies compared to earlier times. This leads to the experience of a serene state of pure consciousness, which is self-evident.

Essence: In the initial stages of devotion, persistent efforts are made, but gradually, as devotion intensifies, everything begins to happen effortlessly. When everything happens effortlessly, and you become aware of your tendencies and defilements, understand that devotion has breached the 51% threshold. Subsequently, a natural and effortless inner transformation unfolds as if something is melting within, leading to the shedding of tendencies and an inner cleansing.

62
The Essence of the Guru

As we intricately string the priceless gems of wisdom received from the Guru, transform them into a string of pearls through contemplation, and offer them for the wellbeing of everyone with the sublime feeling of devotion, life will not only be filled with divine rapture but also brimming with contentment.

Question: I have got to know you through the online discourses delivered by you, and I am also experiencing the miracles of transformation in my life. How can I fully receive and imbibe the Guru essence? How can I always abide in your grace?

Answers: Sirshree (the Guru essence) has already graced you with his presence; it's just that you haven't fully recognized this. For this, you need to sharpen your sword of contemplation. Only with contemplation will you begin to recognize the grace that has been showered upon you at various junctures in life. The sooner you grasp this and train your body-mind, it will become instrumental for the stabilization of the Self.

Through contemplation, your awareness will rise, allowing you to discern the grace being showered in ways that are not obvious at first. To develop this discernment, understand the importance of qualities such as unbiased attentive listening, the detached observation, unyielding willpower, and unwavering focus. Enhance these qualities through consistent experimentation and practice. In doing so, you will realize that the Guru essence always resides within you. The illusion of the Guru's absence arises because you are perceiving through the lens of beliefs.

A person attending a spiritual retreat might believe, "I have acquired knowledge." Conversely, another seeker, not present at the retreat, but deeply engaged in online discourses embraces higher consciousness. They navigate life with profound understanding, perform actions with awareness, and find joy. How is this possible? It occurs because the second person has recognized the Guru essence within himself, even if not consciously aware of it.

Consider a person in prison, unaware of his confinement; They will not contemplate getting out of the prison. In contrast, someone conscious of being in prison actively strives for liberation. Fully recognizing the limitations of the prison, they exert efforts and pray for freedom. This heightened awareness propels them towards liberation.

Do you fully understand your present state? Are you inside the prison of limiting beliefs or have transcended it? Is your life dictated by beliefs, or have you attained freedom?

Reflect on the knowledge you have received today and train your body and mind. Contemplation and practical application of these teachings in your daily life will eventually yield results. Embrace this journey without burden or stress. Keep your happy hat on, preserving your happiness while you tread this path.

> **Essence:** Just as we are all essentially the one consciousness, the Guru, too, is the guiding essence of the same consciousness. The only difference is that consciousness is fully awakened in the Guru. When the Guru's intent reaches us through any medium, we get a glimpse of that consciousness. The darkness within us begins to disappear as we start moving toward the light of higher consciousness.

63
The Essence of Practicing Knowledge

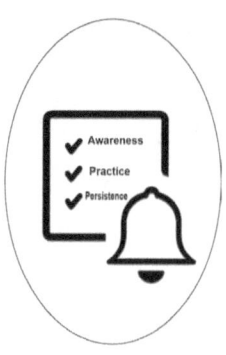

Acquiring knowledge is one thing; putting it into practice is an art. Those who master this art find that even the most challenging tasks become easily manageable, paving the way for success.

Question: Often, despite listening to the Guru, I struggle to put the knowledge into practice. Why does this happen?

Answer: Since childhood, everyone has received worldly knowledge. They see people around them live according to what they have heard and believed and accept that as the gospel truth. This ignorance becomes the cause of bondage, limiting their knowledge.

When one attains the knowledge of the ultimate truth, the mind often raises doubts, "How is this possible?" Instead of focusing on the knowledge received, the mind keeps complaining about what is not happening as expected.

Just ponder, how were you when you had not received this knowledge? Even then, there were aspects understood but not put into practice. Now, after receiving this knowledge, you comprehend some things, yet the mind becomes preoccupied with pointless thoughts like, "How will this happen? Will it practically happen or not?" and continues its unconscious ways.

Hence, practice is essential. Those, who integrated teachings into their lives, consistently practiced them until they seamlessly became an integral part of their nature. Subsequently, their lives became effortless. Upon witnessing the fruits of their practice, they were amazed. They realized its importance in life and wondered, "How can people live without it?"

In the early stages of applying the knowledge received from the Guru, it may seem like nothing significant is happening. Nonetheless, persevere in your practice. Just as regular practice is necessary for improving your handwriting, consistent practice is required to incorporate the knowledge of the truth as an integral part of your nature.

You may not see the results immediately. You may think, "No matter how much I practice, my handwriting isn't improving." However, you may notice gradual improvements in some alphabets, while others, out of habit, persist as before. The change is gradual.

For this, it is essential to start practicing at some point. In some situations, you may find yourself overwhelmed with old doubts and fears, but do not let fear overpower you. When the mind petrifies you, your faith, devotion, and determination will come to your rescue.

Eventually, you will find that what was once a figment of your imagination and prayer has become a reality. While some things have been accomplished, some are yet to happen, so continue practicing. The mind may give excuses to stop the practice. Yet, if you remain detached from the outcome and work with profuse enthusiasm, the knowledge received from the Guru will seamlessly become an integral part of your nature.

Essence: If you attempt to dye a colored cloth with another color, the new color won't hold on to it. In that case, you must wash and remove the earlier color first and then dye the cloth with the new color.

The same principle applies to the knowledge received from the Guru. The Guru, first, cleanses the mind through discourses on the ultimate truth, effectively erasing the old knowledge. Subsequently, the guru imparts new knowledge in its place.

You can mail your opinion or feedback on this book to:
books.feedback@tejgyan.org

About Sirshree

Sirshree's spiritual quest, which began during his childhood, led him on a journey through various schools of philosophy and meditation practices. He studied a wide range of literature on mind science and spirituality. After a long period of deep contemplation on the truth of life, his quest culminated in attaining the ultimate truth.

Sirshree espouses, "All spiritual paths that lead to the truth begin differently but culminate at the same point – Understanding. This understanding is complete in itself. Listening to this understanding is enough to attain the Truth." Over the last two decades, he has dedicated his life to raise mass consciousness.

Sirshree has delivered more than 4000 discourses that throw light on this understanding. He has designed a system for wisdom, which makes it accessible to all. This system has inspired people from all walks of life to progress on their journey of the Truth. Thousands of seekers join in a virtual prayer for World Peace and Global Healing daily at 9:09 am and 9:09 pm.

About Tej Gyan Foundation

Tej Gyan Foundation is a non-profit organization founded on the teachings of Sirshree. The Foundation disseminates Tejgyan – the wisdom that guides one from self-development to Self-realization, leading towards Self-stabilization.

The Foundation's system for imparting wisdom has been assessed by international quality auditors and accredited with the ISO 9001:2015 certification. This wisdom has been presented in a simple, systematic, and practically applicable form that makes it accessible to people from all walks of life, regardless of religion, caste, social strata, country, or belief system.

The Foundation has centers in more than 400 cities and towns across India and other countries. The mission of Tej Gyan Foundation is to create a highly evolved society by leading seekers from negative thoughts to positive thoughts and further, from positive thoughts to Happy thoughts. A 'Happy thought' is the auspicious thought of being free from all thoughts, leading to the state of supreme bliss beyond thoughts.

If you seek such wisdom that leads you beyond mere knowledge, dissolves all problems, frees you from all limiting beliefs, reveals the true nature of divinity, and establishes you in the ultimate truth, then it is time to discover Tejgyan; it is time to rise above the mundane knowledge of words and experience Tejgyan!

The MahaAasmani Magic of Awakening Retreat

Self-development to Self-realization towards Self-stabilization

Do you wish to experience unconditional happiness that is not dependent on any reason? Happiness that is permanent and only increases with time? Do you wish to experience love, peace, self-belief, harmony in relationships, prosperity, and true contentment? Do you wish to progress in all facets of your life, viz. physical, mental, social, financial, and spiritual?

If you seek answers to these questions and are thirsty for the ultimate truth, then you are welcome to participate in the MahaAasmani Magic of Awakening retreat organized by Tej Gyan Foundation. This is the Foundation's flagship retreat based on the teachings of Sirshree.

The purpose of this retreat

Every human being should:

- Discover the answer to "Who am I" and "Why am I?" through direct experience and be established in ultimate bliss.

- Learn the art of living in the present, free from the burden of the past and the anxiety of the future.

- Acquire practical tools to help quieten the chattering mind and dissolve problems.

- Discover missing links in the practices of Meditation (*Dhyana*), Action (*Karma*), Wisdom (*Gyana*), and Devotion (*Bhakti*).

About Books by Sirshree

Sirshree's published work includes more than 150 book titles, some of which have been translated into more than 10 languages. His literature provides a profound reading on various topics of practical living and unravels the missing links in karma, wisdom, devotion, meditation, and consciousness.

His books have been published by leading publishing houses like Penguin, Hay House, Bloomsbury, Wisdom Tree, Jaico, etc. "The Source" book series, authored by Sirshree, has sold over 10 million copies. Various luminaries and celebrities like His Holiness the Dalai Lama, publishers Mr. Reid Tracy, Ms. Tami Simon and Yoga Master Dr. B. K. S. Iyengar have released Sirshree's books and lauded his work.

The Source
Attain Both, Inner Peace
and Worldly success

Awaken the Power of Faith
Discover the 7 Principles of the
Highest Power of the Universe

To order books authored by Sirshree, login to:
www.gethappythoughts.org
For further details, call: +91 9011013210

Tej Gyan Foundation – Contact details

Registered Office:
Happy Thoughts Building, Vikrant Complex, Near Tapovan Mandir, Pimpri, Pune 411017, INDIA. Contact: +91 20-27411240, +91 20-27412576

MaNaN Ashram:
Survey No. 43, Sanas Nagar, Nandoshi Gaon, Kirkatwadi Phata, Off Sinhagad Road, Taluka Haveli, Pune district - 411024, INDIA. Contact: +91 992100 8060.

WORLD PEACE PRAYER

Divine Light of Love, Bliss, and Peace is Showering;

The Golden Light of Higher Consciousness is Rising;

All negativity on Earth is Dissolving;

Everyone is in Peace and Blissfully Shining;

O God, Gratitude for Everything!

Members of Tej Gyan Foundation have been offering this impersonal mass prayer for many years. Those who are happy can offer this prayer. Those feeling low or suffering from illness can receive healing with this prayer.

If you are feeling troubled or sick, please sit to receive the healing effect of this prayer. Visualize that the divine white healing light is being showered on earth through the prayers of thousands and is also reaching you, bringing you peace and good health. You can dwell in this feeling for some time and then offer your gratitude to those offering the prayer.

A Humble Appeal
More than a million peace lovers pray for World Peace and Global Healing every morning and evening at 9:09. Also, a prayer (in Hindi) to elevate consciousness is webcast every day on YouTube at 6:15 am, 3:30 pm and 9:00 pm IST. Please participate in this noble endeavor.

www.ingramcontent.com/pod-product-compliance
Lightning Source LLC
LaVergne TN
LVHW041712070526
838199LV00045B/1320